SHORT SERMONS

FOR

THE CHILDREN'S MASS

BY

REV. FREDERICK REUTER

JOSEPH F. WAGNER

NEW YORK

Nihil Obstat
　　REMIGIUS LAFORT, D.D.
　　　　　Censor

Imprimatur
　　JOHN CARDINAL FARLEY
　　　　　Archbishop of New York

New York, August 11, 1914

Copyright, 1914, by Joseph F. Wagner, New York

DEDICATED

TO MY FRIEND

THE REV. ANTHONY LEININGER

IN HONOR OF HIS

SILVER JUBILEE

PREFACE

GOD has granted me many years in the Holy Priesthood, and during these years I have been active among the young people, endeavoring to teach them how to love and serve God.

When I was a young priest I found it a most difficult task to address the children on Sundays; to bring home to them the Sacred Truths of our Holy Religion in their own language. Many of my brethren in the priesthood are meeting with the same difficulty.

This fact has induced me to gather the sermons which I preached with considerable preparation at children's masses, and to offer them to my fellow workers in the vineyard of the Lord, hoping that they may find them useful in their work.

To hold the attention of children I found that short anecdotes and examples, taken from the lives of Saints and other sources, produced a most wholesome effect. As a consequence I made much use of such illustrative matter, and I believe it forms an important part of these sermons.

The examples and anecdotes are taken from various sources, such as: newspapers, spiritual works, the Lives of the Saints, and books of Catechetical Instructions.

May these Sermons for Children be of some assistance in leading the young folks to God, and in making them understand their obligations in this life, so that thereby they may attain eternal happiness in the hereafter.

THE AUTHOR.

CONTENTS

		PAGE
TWENTY-SIXTH SUNDAY AFTER PENTECOST	Good Example	1
TWENTY-SEVENTH SUNDAY AFTER PENTECOST	Good Intention and Little Things	4
LAST SUNDAY AFTER PENTECOST	Danger of Procrastination	7
FIRST SUNDAY OF ADVENT	The Day of Judgment	11
SECOND SUNDAY OF ADVENT	Fearlessness and Constancy in God's Holy Service	14
THIRD SUNDAY OF ADVENT	The Omnipresence of God	18
FOURTH SUNDAY OF ADVENT	Preparation for Christmas	21
SUNDAY WITHIN THE OCTAVE OF CHRISTMAS	Ingratitude and Bad Example	25
SUNDAY WITHIN THE OCTAVE OF CIRCUMCISION	A Loving Child	29
FIRST SUNDAY AFTER EPIPHANY	Respect to Parents	34
SECOND SUNDAY AFTER EPIPHANY	Marriage, with God and without God	37
THIRD SUNDAY AFTER EPIPHANY	Sin, the Leprosy of the Soul	41
FOURTH SUNDAY AFTER EPIPHANY	The Most Precious Gift — Our Immortal Soul	44
SEPTUAGESIMA SUNDAY	Working out Our Salvation	47
SEXAGESIMA SUNDAY	The Word of God	51
QUINQUAGESIMA SUNDAY	Miserable Condition of the Sinner	54
FIRST SUNDAY IN LENT	On Mortification	58
SECOND SUNDAY IN LENT	Heaven	62
THIRD SUNDAY IN LENT	The Sin of Envy	65
FOURTH SUNDAY IN LENT	Holy Communion	69
PASSION SUNDAY	Sin and Its Consequences	72
PALM SUNDAY	Preparation for Holy Communion	75
EASTER SUNDAY	The State of Grace	78
FIRST SUNDAY AFTER EASTER	God Alone Gives True Peace	81
SECOND SUNDAY AFTER EASTER	The Good Shepherd of the Soul	85
THIRD SUNDAY AFTER EASTER	From Suffering to Joy	89
FOURTH SUNDAY AFTER EASTER	How to Serve God Cheerfully	93

CONTENTS

		PAGE
FIFTH SUNDAY AFTER EASTER	Prayer	96
SUNDAY WITHIN THE OCTAVE OF THE ASCENSION	The Spirit of Truth	99
PENTECOST	Courage for the Love of the Lord	103
FIRST SUNDAY AFTER PENTECOST	Works of Mercy	107
SECOND SUNDAY AFTER PENTECOST	A Royal Banquet	111
THIRD SUNDAY AFTER PENTECOST	The Erring Sheep	115
FOURTH SUNDAY AFTER PENTECOST	The Word of God and the Word of Parents	118
FIFTH SUNDAY AFTER PENTECOST	Hypocrisy. Charity Towards Our Neighbor	122
SIXTH SUNDAY AFTER PENTECOST	The Holy Sacrifice of the Mass	126
SEVENTH SUNDAY AFTER PENTECOST	Scandal	129
EIGHTH SUNDAY AFTER PENTECOST	The Fruit of Almsgiving	132
NINTH SUNDAY AFTER PENTECOST	The Obstinate Sinner. The House of God	136
TENTH SUNDAY AFTER PENTECOST	Pride	139
ELEVENTH SUNDAY AFTER PENTECOST	Impenitence	142
TWELFTH SUNDAY AFTER PENTECOST	The Sin of Slander	145
THIRTEENTH SUNDAY AFTER PENTECOST	A Cancer of the Soul	148
FOURTEENTH SUNDAY AFTER PENTECOST	Seek First the Kingdom of God	152
FIFTEENTH SUNDAY AFTER PENTECOST	Homeward Bound	155
SIXTEENTH SUNDAY AFTER PENTECOST	Sanctifying the Lord's Day	159
SEVENTEENTH SUNDAY AFTER PENTECOST	On Intimate Terms with God	162
EIGHTEENTH SUNDAY AFTER PENTECOST	The Interest of Our Lord Paramount	166
NINETEENTH SUNDAY AFTER PENTECOST	The Royal Banquet Hall of God	170
TWENTIETH SUNDAY AFTER PENTECOST	The Gift of Faith	174
TWENTY-FIRST SUNDAY AFTER PENTECOST	Forgiving Injuries	179
TWENTY-SECOND SUNDAY AFTER PENTECOST	The Gift of God — What belongs to God'	183
TWENTY-THIRD SUNDAY AFTER PENTECOST	Obstinacy in Sin	187

SERMONS FOR THE CHILDREN'S MASS

TWENTY-SIXTH SUNDAY AFTER PENTECOST

Good Example

Those of you, my dear children, who live in a city, have probably no idea of a farmer's field. Yet it is to the avocation of the farmer that our Divine Lord directs our attention to-day. His duty it is to till the soil and prepare it for the seed; his duty, to scatter that seed, not in the desert places, but in the land that he has been cultivating.

Our Lord, my children, is doing the same kind of work as the farmer, but it is the cultivation and the sowing of good seed in your hearts, that comprises His lifework, not the tillage of the earth. Holy thoughts and inspirations, holy desires to do what is right, constitute the good seed that will take deep root in the soil of your hearts if you only wish it. See that you place no obstacle in the way of its growth—but rather that you continue God's work by sowing the seed in other souls, and nourishing it carefully by the sunshine of good example.

An old general was one day asked by a friend, how it was that after spending so many years in camp, he yet perservered in frequent Communion. His friend deemed camplife not conducive to the upbuilding of religious principles. But the general answered, "My friend, would you believe that the strangest thing of it all is that my conversion was brought about before I ever heard the word of a priest? When my campaign was over, God gave me a pious wife whose faith I respected but did not share. Before I married her, she was a member of the Sodality of the Children of Mary in her parish, and I noticed that no matter what she was writing, she never failed to add to her signature 'Child of Mary.' After our marriage, she never took it upon herself to lecture me about God, but she did not cease her prayers, nevertheless. Night and morning saw her on her knees, and when she came home from Mass on Sundays, there was a quiet sweetness about her, so that to me she seemed like an angel. Suddenly I myself was attracted by the God she loved so well. I desired to know more of Him, and soon, I, who had been a complete stranger to the practice of religion, I sought my wife and said to her 'Take me to your confessor.' That was the beginning of my conversion, my friend. Through the ministrations of that good man, I am what I am to-day."

How productive, my dear children, has been that good seed sown by the Divine Husbandman, through the ministry of the general's wife. So, too, may you influence others by your piour behavior and good example. But young people, unfortunately, often permit the sower of cockle to enter their hearts. The devil employs his arts to make his evil work look insignificant, and he succeeds only too well. A slight consent to the wrong, that is all he wants.

St. Augustine relates a story about a young friend of his, Alpius by name, who went to Rome to pursue his studies. It was customary for the young men of Rome to amuse themselves by going to public shows. On one occasion, Alpius was forced, against his will, to accompany some of his friends to one of these places of amusement. He was, however, resolved to close his eyes that no sinful scene might imprint itself on his soul. But, sad to relate, he forgot to close his *ears,* and thus sin entered his heart.

About the middle of the performance, the audience began to shout and applaud loudly. Alpius forgot his resolution. Opening his eyes, he was attracted by the scene, and so he continued to gaze till the play was finished.

Night after night saw Alpius again in the theatre. Unmindful alike of his prayers and his studies, he soon became worse than any of his companions. Though it is gratifying to relate that Alpius, through the supplications of St. Augustine, again returned to the path of duty, still this example ought to warn you, my dear children, how readily the devil may ensnare you in small things.

It is true that God's mercy is unlimited, but when the harvest-time draws nigh, the Almighty will give His orders to His angels to separate the cockle from the wheat. Then, indeed, will the cockle—the youths that ridicule religion and holy things—be gathered into bundles to burn. How many knowing of this final reckoning day of God care very little about it, and continue in their evil ways!

Be not hardened, therefore, in your hearts, my dear children, but heed the threats of an angry God. All your life, endeavor to be models of good example. Thus only will you be reckoned by the reapers at the harvest-time as the precious wheat that is to be gathered into our Father's barn.

TWENTY-SEVENTH SUNDAY AFTER PENTECOST

Good Intention and Little Things

My dear children: You will notice, if you read the history of our Lord's beautiful life, that He lays great stress on little things. In to-day's Gospel, He speaks of a mustard seed, "which is the least indeed of all seeds, but when it is grown up, it is greater than all herbs, and becometh a tree." Why does our Lord choose the mustard seed in preference to all others? Listen, my Children: He wants to show us that we are not obliged to do great things to gain heaven, but that the little duties of every-day life, if well performed, will win for us a happy Eternity.

As soon as you arise in the morning, make the sign of the Cross, and offer all your thoughts, words and actions to God. During the day, often think of God, even while you are amusing yourself. At night, raise your heart once more to Him before retiring. Thus will you make your day one for heaven rather than for time.

When the holy Curé of Ars was a little boy, he had to work in the fields because of the poverty of his father. He, however, offered all his manual labor to Jesus. "Alone in the fields," he writes, "I often spoke to Jesus aloud; but when companions were with me, I prayed to Him in my heart. After dinner, before we began work again, we had a short rest. Then, though I stretched myself on the ground like the others, I was all the time praying to Jesus with my whole soul. Oh! how happy those days were!". Only little moments offered to God—little works performed for Him—but what an increase of merit in heaven have they not procured for that holy, humble saint!

Our good Lord Himself promises a hundredfold reward to anyone who gives but a glass of water in His Name, while St. Francis de Sales urges us, "My children, perhaps you will never have it in your power to do great works for God, but little ones you can perform every day of your lives. He who lays a brick upon a building, each succeeding day, will soon complete a large house. Do some good, therefore, every moment of your lives."

It is related that a great saint was one day playing a game of ball. In the midst of the game one of his companions said: "I wonder what we would do if we were to die this minute." One answered: "I would kneel down and say my prayers." Another said: "I would immediately go to Confession." A third ventured "I would run to the nearest church." As it was now the saint's turn to speak, he smilingly said: "And I would just go on with my game." The others exclaimed in surprise: "Oh! father, how could you prepare yourself to die that way?" But the saint quietly made answer: "I began this game with the intention of pleasing God, and, therefore, I am doing what is most agreeable to Him."

A little thing—a simple game—and yet an act of worship to the All-powerful God! How grateful we ought to be that God is content to take the insignificant actions of every-day life, and make them current coin for eternity!

There is another inducement why we ought to surrender our whole heart and soul to the right performance of little things—they often bring souls near to God. Acts of charity unselfishly performed, regular attendance at church on Sundays, due observation of the days of abstinence—all these are little things that may turn souls from the evil of their ways, and lead them to the Heavenly Kingdom. What greater reward could we have than this?

There was once a soldier who, having been wounded in battle, was sick unto death. A Catholic army chaplain, hearing of his condition, sought him on the battlefield. When the priest came to the spot where the poor man was lying, he tried to comfort him in his distress, and asked him what he could do for him. "Give me a bundle of straw on which to rest my body," said the soldier. In a few moments the priest returned with the straw, and having placed the dying man comfortably upon it, inquired, "Is there anything else I can do for you?" "Yes," replied the soldier, "please bring me some wine, that I may take some refreshment before I die." Soon the priest was back on his knees, moistening the parched lips. As the clergyman was about to go away, feeling that he had done everything in his power, the soldier said, "Father, I desire one thing more of you. I want to become a Catholic, for the religion that teaches such charity as yours does, must surely be the true religion." The priest, overjoyed at this unlooked-for grace, had the happiness of baptizing the dying man, and of seeing him depart this life in God's love and friendship. All these, my children, were but little acts of charity on the part of the priest, and yet, see how they saved a soul!

Only after death shall you realize how much little things count in the sight of God. That Mass which you attended with devotion, that kind deed which seemed to be of no great consequence, were perhaps the beginning of God's special grace for you. Truly, it is because people think little of God and despise small things, that so many are lost for all eternity.

TWENTY-EIGHTH AND LAST SUNDAY AFTER PENTECOST

Danger of Procrastination

"Heaven and earth shall pass away, but My words shall not pass away."

The last Gospel of the ecclesiastical year, my dear little children, lies open before us. Patiently and lovingly have we listened Sunday after Sunday to our dear Lord's words. Now we have laid the wounds and wants of our souls before Him—and again we have been enthroned on His knee, and heard the gentle pleading of His Sacred Human Heart; "Suffer the little children." And we have loved *our* particular corner in His Heart! Grown-ups may do great things for Him which we could never do—but we, His little children, can love as much as they. And we *do* love Him, don't we? Yet it is not His gentle, tender aspect that the Church on this last Sunday of her year, puts before us. We hear dread words to-day—words that the little ones hardly understand. And yet we know it is something mighty, something fearful that is going to take place, else why should our Lord warn us? But God grant that we do not live to see those days—God grant that when the shadows close over our little earth for the last time, we may have been long ago gathered to our fathers. Still this awe-inspiring Gospel has a lesson for us also. Will the day ever come when we shall wander away from the path of truth? God forbid—yet it is well for us to think of what might happen under those circumstances to the dear little souls entrusted to our charge. What might the "abomination of desolation" mean for us? Suppose we have sinned, sinned grievously—and that we vainly put off our conversion till the last day of our lives. What will God do? Perhaps He will let us die impenitent, and thus become the victims of eternal damnation. He who lives a bad life will die a bad death. "As the tree falls, so will it lie." But, thank God, my children, this is still only a supposition for us. "Now is the acceptable time; now is the day of Salvation." Let us lay the foundation of our new spiritual edifice on the fear of God. If we fear, we shall beware; if we beware, we shall save our souls. The saints fasted, toiled and wept, not only because of the love they bore their Master, but also because of their fear of damnation. In comparison with these, how shall we, with our self-indulgent lives and lax conscience, dare to face the judgment-seat of God?

In the life of St. Louis, we read that no amount of penances could satisfy his deep fear of the judgments of God, and that frequently at night, after a day of unintermitting toil, the thought of the uncertainty of his Salvation would make him tremble violently.

There was once a young man who in his childhood was very pious, but as he mingled with the world, he relinquished his religious practices and fell into grievous sin. Yet he always consoled himself with the thought: "Never would I die without the Sacraments. That would be a serious wrong offered to God. But I am young yet, and I cannot at present make up my mind to go to Confession. There is plenty of time. God is good and merciful."

The day came all too soon, however, when he lay dying. His good mother, smoothing his pillow, bent over him and exhorted him to make his peace with God. Gently he answered her: "Yes, my mother, I know I must change my life. Evil habits have gotten the better of me. Yet the strain might be too much for me now. Let me wait till I recover my health."

"But you are in danger of death, my son," she insisted. "Won't you make your Confession now, lest you might never get well again?"

In response to her urgent entreaties, he at last consented that she should send for the priest. Unfortunately, it happened that the latter was absent from home at the time, on another sick call. When he did reach the youth's bedside, it was too late—all was over: he had died in despair.

Sooner or later, my dear children, our good God gives every sinner, no matter how wayward, a chance to return to Him. His own Words are: "I seek not the death of the sinner, but that he should be converted and live." For the erring child He does more than the father of the prodigal. He follows him to the far land where he is wasting his substance. But even God's mercy has a limit. The day may come when He turns away and leaves the wanderer to persist in his wicked madness.

Years ago, a young man named Theodore, was sent to one of the monasteries of Italy, to be educated. However, instead of leading the holy life outlined for the inmates of the house, he yielded to the weaknesses of his nature, and surrendered his heart to worldly enjoyments. In the midst of his evil career, he was suddenly struck down by the hand of God. A plague, then devastating Rome, numbered him as one of its victims, and it seemed all the vitality of his youth would not be proof against the ravages of the disease. One day, while the monks were gathered around his bedside, he caused terror in the hearts of all by exclaiming: "Go away from me; leave me to my fate; I am already delivereth to the Evil One. See, he has even now begun to torture me with his fiery breath."

The good monks, pitying the state of the young man, tried to encourage him in the following words: "O brother, what are you saying? Arm yourself with the sign of the Cross, that the enemy of souls may leave you in peace." But the dying youth sorrowfully answered: "I cannot. My very arms seem immovable." Then with sighs and supplications, the monks earnestly begged this precious soul of God. He was one of their number: would not the Almighty spare him? At last Theodore grew calm. His face assumed a gentler expression. The worst of the combat was over. Lifting his eyes and casting them on his brethren, he softly murmured: "Thanks to God, the Evil One has left me. Frightened by your prayers, he took to flight. But what a lesson I have learned! How terrible it is to fall into the hands of the All-holy God after a life spent in forgetfulness of Him. Oh! let me be converted and live!" He was true to his resolve, for having been restored to health, he became a sincere penitent and died the death of a saint.

My dear little children, one word more. Do not think that you can possess God in Eternity without loving Him on earth. And you know the signs of love you must show Him; pray to Him trustingly, seek Him often in the Holy Sacrament of the Altar, be a real child to Him, receive Him and clasp Him to your heart in frequent Communion—and doing all this, do you think that He will resist your appeals, or reject your love? Ah! no, never! Not only will He joyfully claim in this life every pulsation of the dear little heart beating only for Him, but in the life to come He will press you to His bosom for all Eternity!

FIRST SUNDAY OF ADVENT

The Day of Judgment

Little ones, dear to the heart of God, it is to you I would speak to-day: to you I would appeal on this first Sunday of Advent, when the Church enters upon a new season of the ecclesiastical year. What is it I would have you do? Only this: to prepare your little hearts for the coming of the dear Infant Jesus at Christmas—for Advent, you know, means "coming." During these four weeks we should direct our thoughts to that great mystery—Jesus become a little Babe for us—and prepare ourselves worthily for His abiding with us.

Now, let us see what great lesson our holy mother the Church teaches us in her Gospel of to-day. It is true, Our Lord did come to earth once as a little child, yet, He is going to come again, not as a helpless babe, but as a King in all glory and majesty. Then He will judge each one of us for all the good and evil we have done—and so the Church to-day tells us of that dread Day of Judgment.

Have we not, young as we are, committed sins for which God will punish us? Even the saints, though they were holy men and women, feared the final judgment. On one occasion that great servant of God, St. Mary Magdalen of Pazzi, being very sick, sent in haste for her confessor.

"Father," she exclaimed, as soon as she saw him coming, "I have been thinking about the terrible Judgment of God; I am frightened. Do you think that I will be saved?" Unhesitatingly the good priest answered: "I have the fullest confidence that heaven will be your home. Why are you fretting?" "God's judgments are so different from ours," she said, "and my time is coming soon when I shall stand alone before my Judge, to be examined on everything I have said or done in my whole life."

Dear children, Mary Magdalen was a saint who all her life walked in the presence of God, and yet, see how she feared to stand before the All-holy. But how few we find in the world to-day, leading the lives of saints! Nevertheless, all must die and face that last judgment. How they will tremble when they see themselves, condemned, perhaps, forever!

My dear boys and girls, I cannot find words strong enough to impress on your minds, how you ought to strive from day to day to be good children and become more pleasing to God. St. Jerome often struck his breast with a stone, thus causing the blood to flow, and when asked why he did this, he said: "Whenever I think of God's Judgment, I begin to tremble, whether I eat or drink or do anything else."

My children, what will the Judge have to say to us when we appear before Him? Perhaps He will have reason to chide us in these words: "So far I have been patient and silent, but now is My time to punish you. You arose in the morning and went to bed at night without saying your prayers. Nay more, you even learned to take My Name in vain. You went to church to do naught but dishonor Me, for, during Holy Mass you laughed and talked and did not pray. See how disobedient you were to your parents and superiors, contrary to My express command. You even led others into sin, and for their souls you must answer as well as for your own. Where are the graces of your first Holy Communion? Gone, all gone! Now, God's anger must be appeased. Depart from My sight forever!" Such are the words our Divine

Judge shall speak to us if we disregard His Law and trifle with His Commandments.

It is related by St. Vincent that a young man once had a dream in which he saw himself standing before the tribunal of God. So terrible was the scene he witnessed, that when he awoke he was trembling and was covered with a cold sweat. Immediately he thanked Jesus that his dream was not a reality. But he thought within himself: "What I have seen in my sleep will at some future time actually occur. Perhaps it may be soon, even this very day." Thereupon he asked God to forgive him, and promised from that hour to lead a life of penance. So great was the effect of this dream that the young man grew sad and grave in disposition, while his hair became white as snow.

What this youth did, you too can do, my dear children: Lead a life of penance and rather die than commit sin. Thus you will prepare yourselves for the coming of your Lord. During this holy season, you can do so much to please the dear Infant Jesus: arise in the morning at the first call and assist at Holy Mass; be obedient to your parents, kind to your little companions, etc.

What a lovely, pure heart you will then present to the Lord Jesus for His crib! What matter that the people of Bethlehem did not receive Him so long ago, if only, way back in this twentieth century, there are little hearts longing for His company. Keep then your soul all pure for Him, not only now, but throughout your whole life, and, if you do this, you may entertain the surest hope that you will meet a most merciful Judge when you die.

SECOND SUNDAY OF ADVENT

Fearlessness and Constancy in God's Holy Service

My Dear Children: To-day's Gospel presents to us a man who is a type of courage and fearlessness in God's holy service—none other than St. John the Baptist, the one chosen by God from all eternity to prepare the way of the Lord and make straight His paths.

At the time that St. John began his holy mission, Herod, a very wicked man, was ruler in the land of Judea. So far no one had had the courage to reprove him for his crimes, but John could not see the good God offended and remain inactive. He went to Herod and in vigorous language pointed out to him the error of his ways. Though the king may have realized the truth of John's arguments, still all the return the Baptist received for his fearlessness was condemnation to a loathsome prison.

There are few men to-day, my children, possessing the least spark of the courage of St. John, for if there were, the world would be far better than it is. To all succeeding ages he is the model of zeal for the glory of God, the model of fearlessness in repressing vice. You, too, my children, though you may never be called upon to do the great deeds of a John the Baptist, yet you have numberless opportunities of defending God's Holy Name. It is in your power to take God's part everywhere; in the street, at home, in company—wherever there is a gathering of boys and girls, or even men and women.

Would you like to hear a story of a little girl, who, although very young, had learned from her dear mother the knowledge and love of God? Well, one day she happened to be at dinner with a large number of people who were strangers to her. Among these were two young men fashionably dressed and apparently of good society. Hardly had the dinner commenced when they began to speak irreverently of God, and take His Holy Name in vain. At this the little girl was very much displeased, and she looked to the grown-up folks for one who had courage enough to bid them be silent. Finally, when the child saw that no one checked them, she rose from her place, and quietly going over to them, said, "Gentlemen, it is not right for you to speak that way. No one ought to speak of God in that manner. Indeed, it is very wrong of you." The reproof struck home. Astonished to hear these words from the lips of a mere child, the young men flushed and said no more. Shortly after they left the table in disgrace, beaten by the courage of a little girl.

You can do the same, my children. Let no one speak irreverently of God in your presence. Should your father at home curse or swear, put your little arms around his neck sometime, and whisper, so that only he will hear the gentle words: "Father, it isn't nice to swear or curse. Don't you know that it offends God, and that you thereby commit a great sin?" If you have parents who do not attend Mass on Sundays, or who neglect to go to Communion at Easter time, ask them for God's sake and the sake of their immortal souls, to attend to their religious duties.

I know of a young boy, who, on his First Communion Day, felt a tinge of sadness because his parents neglected holy Mass on Sundays. He had begged them so often to go, but all in vain. Now, however, he made up his mind to pray unceasingly for them. On two mornings of every week he attended Mass, offering it for his parents' conversion. Soon his mother noticed that he went out regularly at a certain hour. Determined to learn what her boy was doing, she followed him one day, and, entering the church, saw him kneeling before the altar, praying with the greatest fervor. Patiently she waited, till the "Ita missa est" of the priest, which she had not heard for years, told her the Mass was finished. Tears were in the boy's eyes as he left the church, but what was his surprise when he found his mother waiting for him at the door. When she asked him what was the cause of his sorrow, he threw his arms around her and said: "Yesterday it was for father, and to-day, mother, it was for you." The result of the boy's fervent prayer and self-sacrifice was that God touched these two hearts with His grace, so that the following Sunday father and mother accompanied their devoted child to Mass. My children, this little boy is a beautiful example for you.

How can you show your love for Christ better than by being a good Christian, not in name only, but in deed? The true Christian is one who does good works and leads a sinless life. By his conduct the great St. John showed that he was a true follower of Christ, and that is the reason why he drew so many souls to God. St. John, too, was firm. No one could lead him from the path of duty, either by flattery, threats, or even death. Compare your attitude with his in this respect. How often, my children, do you not resolve to keep away from bad company, but alas! how often do you not return to it again.

See how firm St. Agnes was when she feared not even the executioner who was to put her to death. She was but a child, yet, having made up her mind to serve God, nothing could make her untrue to her determination. This child saint teaches us, my dear children, how to be firm and constant in God's holy service.

Our one object in life must be to advance God's glory in spite of all opposition, and thus by our firmness and constancy we shall share, with St. John the Baptist and St. Agnes, the joy of the Eternal Reward.

THIRD SUNDAY OF ADVENT

The Omnipresence of God

Again to-day does the Church bring St. John the Baptist before our minds, my dear children. Priests and Levites have come from Jerusalem to ask him who he is, and because they have been giving him too much renown and slighting our Divine Lord, he reproves them severely. Although Jesus was constantly among them, yet they knew Him not. Do you not notice, children, that many of us often act like the Jews? We are always in God's presence, but how frequently do we forget this. What holy reverence should we not have for the adorable majesty of God!

We are told that, in her youth, St. Thais was leading a very wicked life, and God inspired the holy abbot Paphnutius to undertake her conversion. Accordingly, dressed as a wealthy man, he went to visit her. On being admitted to her house, he requested to speak to her. Thais showed him a room where they would not be disturbed, but the abbot asked for a more retired spot. As he was still dissatisfied when another room was shown him, Thais said: "No one can possibly see or hear us here." "But what about God?" said Paphnutius. "Is there no place where we can escape His all-seeing Eye?" "Alas! no," replied Thais, casting herself at his feet, for she now perceived in him the man of God. In consequence she abandoned her wicked career for a life of penance in the desert.

My children, would you not be ashamed to commit sin in the presence of your parents or friends? Why do you look for dark places if not that you may be hidden from their eyes? And yet you forget there is One greater than parents and friends who sees you always —God, your Father, Who loves you—God, your Judge, to Whom you must one day give an account of all your actions, and Who at any moment can cast you into hell.

A young man once went to a holy priest and said to him: "Father, I am constantly tormented with bad thoughts, but I am most anxious to banish them from my mind." "My child," replied the priest, "if your head were made of glass, so that everyone could see these thoughts, how long to you think would you entertain them?" "Oh! I would put them away at once," answered the youth, "for I would feel very much ashamed." "Then remember," said the priest, "that God sees every one of your thoughts as clearly as if they were covered by thin transparent glass. When these evil desires come to your mind, say to yourself: 'God sees me,' and immediately the recollection of His presence will dispel the allurements of sense."

When you, my dear children, are tempted to sin or to do evil, say to yourself: "God sees me, that same God who will one day judge me." If you would make use of these words habitually, you would always live a holy, happy life. Think thus within yourself: I stand in the presence of God. He sees me! What a great desire then I ought to have to perform my duties well! If Almighty God is looking at me, must I not recite my prayers with devotion and reverence? Must I not say, whatever the Cross He send me, "Lord, Thy will be done!"

During her lifetime, St. Lidwina was afflicted with very severe sufferings. Her body was covered with sores, and for thirty-eight years she had to lie on a hard bed. Being deprived of sufficient covering on account of her poverty, she suffered much from the extreme cold. People abused her and even struck her, yet, despite all her sufferings, both of mind and body, she never complained, but was always patient and resigned. Her one thought was, "God sees and knows all. That is sufficient for me."

And so it ought to be sufficient for you, too, my dear children. Walk ever in the presence of God, and you will avoid sin. When you arise in the morning, raise your heart to Him. During the day, no matter what you are doing, remember that God's eye is upon you. If you thus walk in His holy presence during life, you may rest assured that you will enjoy Him face to face for all eternity.

FOURTH SUNDAY OF ADVENT

Preparation for Christmas

"Prepare ye the way of the Lord, make straight His paths."

Only a few more days are left, my dear children, and the joyous Christmas feast will be here—the anniversary of our dear Lord's coming into this world.

Did you ever notice how, when the President of the United States plans visiting a large city, the people, some days before begin to clean the streets and decorate their houses with bunting and flags? Now, if such deference is paid to an earthly ruler, my children, what ought we think of the coming of the King of Kings? So, during the holy season of Advent, we are reminded continually that there is some one coming to visit us—someone far greater than the President of the United States, or any such dignitary—our Divine Lord and Saviour, Jesus Christ. No wonder St. John cries out with all the fervor of his heart: "Prepare ye the way of the Lord, make straight His paths." No wonder that he urges us: "Do penance, for the kingdom of heaven is at hand." Therefore the good Christian carefully prepares his heart, knowing that the great God so soon to be born amongst us pleads thus with us: "My child, give Me thy heart. As My kingdom is not of this world, it is vain and fruitless for you to expect to have here a lasting stay. Look to heaven for your future home, and prepare by a good life for joys unspeakable."

During these weeks of Advent, my dear children, one figure has stood out prominently in the Gospels of Holy Mother

Church, and that one is John the Baptist. St. John was a man of rigorous self-denial; his entire manner of living was one of consummate penance, and not only did he adopt this mode of life for himself, but he urged others also to follow his example. Can we not walk in his footsteps, at least in a slight degree, my children? It is true that we are not obliged to perform the penances that were his daily portion, but there is one thing we can do, and ought to do—we should humble ourselves at this holy season and make a good Confession. It is more than strange how many of us, my dear boys and girls, do not want to make use of this means of grace, by which we become once more the dear children of God, after we have offended Him by sin. Let us go to Confession, then, humbly and sincerely, and not be afraid to tell our sins, whatever they may be. The more sincere and heartfelt we are, the more God loves us.

It is related that a young man once went to Confession to St. Francis de Sales, and after having confessed with genuine sorrow the great offences he had committed against God, he said to the Saint: "Father, what do you think of me when you hear such enormous sins?" "My son," answered the holy man, embracing him, "what do I think of you? I think that you are a saint. A moment ago you were God's enemy, but now the Almighty has pardoned you and made you one of His elect."

My children, if you should ever feel ashamed to confess any sin you have committed, have immediate recourse to prayer to overcome the difficulty. And why should you be averse to confess that which you were not ashamed to commit?

A young girl had, on one occasion, been guilty of a grievous offence against God, which she failed to confess because of shame. For eight years she allowed that burden to remain on her conscience, and though she knew it was a mortal sin, she received the Sacraments repeatedly. At last, on one of our Blessed Mother's feasts she went to church, as was her wont, and kneeling at the altar of her who is "Our tainted nature's solitary boast," she gained the strength and courage needful for complete conversion. She rose from her knees a changed girl. She confessed her sin, and lived the rest of her life like a real saint.

Many children there are, and even adults, who go to Confession, it is true, as the Church requires, but who, unfortunately, frequent the tribunal of penance without true sorrow for sin. Perhaps they do not wish to give up association with a bad companion, or do not intend to quit an evil habit, and consequently they make a bad Confession.

The following significant story is told by a good missionary father. A young girl received Holy Communion on a certain Easter Sunday. Having returned to her place, she knelt there apparently communing with her Lord devoutly, when suddenly, to the astonishment of all, she swooned away. Kind hands soon raised her and carried her to the nearest house. Holy Mass being finished, the priest went immediately to see the sick girl. He looked into the pale face before him, but no sign of recognition lighted the ghastly eyes. While the holy man stood there wondering what ailed the young girl, she suddenly exclaimed: "This morning I made a bad Communion, for in my Confession yesterday I concealed a great sin which I was afraid to tell." Saying this she expired before the priest could offer her a word of encouragement. With this example before your eyes, my dear children, I beg of you never to be afraid to confess the sins you have committed, and always have a great sorrow for your sins.

"Prepare the way of the Lord" then, my children, by receiving the Sacrament of Penance worthily, and by ornamenting your souls with solid virtue—above all, the virtues of purity and charity. With St. Augustine, say: "I love Thee, my God, and I desire to love Thee more."

We must all do as the Saints did when they prepared themselves for the holy feast of Christmas: They prayed more fervently and frequently; they were more charitable to all with whom they came in contact, and in every possible manner they adorned their souls with virtue.

O Jesus, sweet Babe of Bethlehem, come, make Your Throne in our poor hearts. At least, we will shelter You from the cold of the winter night, and by our love endear ourselves to You. We need much, dear Jesus, so much for our present needs, so much for our future life. Come, fill our souls with Your grace, and keep us always true to You. Then surely, in Your company, sweet Babe of Bethlehem, we shall enjoy a holy and blessed Christmas.

SUNDAY WITHIN THE OCTAVE OF CHRISTMAS

Ingratitude and Bad Example

My Dear Children: Christmas, pre-eminently the feast of the little ones of God's house, with all its heavenly glory and tender memories, has passed away, but we may still pay a visit to the dear Infant Jesus in His crib, and give our hearts into His safe keeping. As we look at Him lying there on His bed of straw, He seems to smile in spite of all the discomforts that surround His birthplace. Could He have chosen a poorer dwelling on His entrance into life? Who of us was ever born in a stable? From the very first moment that He opened His little eyes on this world, the Child Jesus began to suffer for us, and He suffered with untold joy, for the Cross was God's way of reopening heaven for poor fallen man.

But, my dear children, how many people in the world to-day remember the great love that Jesus showed from the very beginning of His mortal life? Carelessly they follow their appointed ways, not in the least affected by the sacrifices He has offered for them. Ah! what an ungrateful return is made to Him, even by those who ought to love Him most.

To show you how man's base ingratitude grieves the dear Heart of the Infant Jesus, let me tell you a little story: One night, in the midst of a winter of long ago, a certain holy monk was traveling through a forest. While on his journey he was thinking about the love of the good God for us in sending His Divine Son to redeem the world. Suddenly the cries of a child, evidently not far away, attracted his attention. Turning in the direction from whence the sound came he saw lying on the snow a beautiful little boy, crying and trembling with cold. Filled with compassion for the poor little one, he said: "My child, how is it that you are thus left alone this cold winter's night? And why are you crying?" To which the boy answered: "Alas! how can I help crying when I see myself abandoned by everyone, when nobody receives me or has pity upon me!" With these words the child disappeared. The monk then understood that the vision he had seen was to teach him that men, instead of loving the Jesus who came from heaven to save them, gave Him no room in their hearts.

My children, did you notice those words spoken by the holy old man, Simeon, about the Infant Jesus, as recorded in to-day's Gospel? "Behold this Child is set for the fall and for the resurrection of many in Israel." What a heart-stirring prophecy! To whom will this Child be a "fall," a ruin? He will be a ruin to those who will not believe in Him; He will be a ruin to many Christians who are only Christians in name; He will be a ruin to those who offend and blaspheme God; and He will be a ruin to those who, by their bad example, lead others astray. What will He be to us—a fall or a resurrection?

A pious man living in the thirteenth century tells of a noble youth whose life was blighted by the example of a bad companion. A good, holy mother and father had reared him in the knowledge and fear of God. When he was approaching manhood his parents sent him to college, thinking thereby to make their son better fitted for the place he should occupy in the world. But alas! among his college friends there was one who was corrupt at heart, one who exercised his fatal sway over the innocent youth, till he had made him corrupt like himself—irreligious, criminal. Piteously did his parents plead with him to leave this dangerous companion, to return once more to the pious practices of his youth, but all in vain.

Some time after he contracted a painful disease which left him no hope of recovery. In distress a good priest visited him to see if he could administer any comfort to the dying man. All seemed useless. One word was ever on his lips: "Woe to him who led me astray!" Softly the priest tried to quiet him and promised him that God would, in His goodness and mercy, forgive him if he would repent. But the young man replied: "It is useless to ask God to forgive me. Too late would come my pardon. Oh! woe to that one who led me astray!" Saying these words the unhappy man died in an agony of despair.

My children, this example ought to rouse you to resolve to be never in all your lives guilty of leading anyone into sin.

There is another consideration that ought to induce you to avoid all sin. Not only is the doing of evil an offence to God, but it also grieves the heart of His Most Blessed Mother. As any earthly mother would resent an injury offered to her Son, so Mary is pained when we live as though we had no dependence on Jesus.

In the life of St. Lutgard, we read how the Blessed Virgin, on one occasion, appeared to the saint. Struck by the sadness of her countenance, Lutgard lovingly asked her the cause of her grief. Mary replied: "How can I be joyful when so many crucify my most Holy Son every day?"

And St. Alphonsus tells that when we sin we take the hammer from the executioners of Our Divine Lord, and once more drive the cruel nails through His sacred hands and feet. Then, as if not satisfied with our impious work, we plunge the sword of sorrow deep into Mary's soul.

In conclusion, let me exhort you, my dear children, if you love Jesus, avoid sin; if you love our Blessed Mother, keep far away from its occasions. Only by such efforts will you merit the smile of the Son and the Mother, in time and eternity.

SUNDAY WITHIN THE OCTAVE OF CIRCUMCISION

A Loving Child

My dear Children: In your Bible History you have learned how the good St. Joseph had to take the Blessed Virgin and the Divine Child to Egypt. It was on account of Herod, who wanted to kill Jesus.

During the sojourn of the Holy Family in that strange country, St. Joseph did every thing a good father could do for a child. After the death of Herod an angel appeared and commanded him to return into his own country. He obeyed, took the Child and His Mother and came into the land of Israel. This great solicitude on the part of the foster father of our dear Lord reminds us of the great care which pious parents take of their children, in order to protect them from their numerous enemies. Your welfare, children, is the dearest object of your parents' care, for which you owe them your heartfelt gratitude; but since you are not able to thank them for it as they deserve, you should at least love them from the bottom of your heart.

I am going to tell you why you should love your parents.

First of all it is an instinct implanted in us by nature. Did you ever observe what tender feelings not only domestic animals but also wild beasts show towards their parents. This instinct is imparted to them by their Creator. See the little child how it smiles upon its mother. Just think, dear children, what a monster is a boy or girl who acts against this natural impulse.

Furthermore, we are often put to shame by the heathens and the Gentiles who simply followed the natural law. Pliny the Younger, who was a Roman and a heathen, at the risk of his own life saved his mother from burning to death, at the time of the great eruption of Mt. Vesuvius in the southern part of Italy. Will a Christian boy or girl suffer a Gentile to surpass them in this virtue? Listen to the words of Holy Scripture: "He that afflicteth his father, and chaseth away his mother, is infamous and unhappy."

Children, you all remember the fourth Commandment: "Honor thy father and thy mother." Here you see, it is a Command from God to love your parents. God says in another place: "Son, support the old age of thy father, and grieve him not in his life." To those who love their parents God has promised great rewards. "He that honored his father shall have joy in his own children; and in the day of his prayer he shall be heard." And do you know, children, God has kept His promises; in the old Law we find a multitude of examples. There was Isaac, Jacob and Joseph, who loved their parents sincerely; they enjoyed in this world a long, contented and happy life. You all know how Joseph was rewarded by becoming the first man of the country in which he lived, he was placed next to the king.

History relates an incident in the life of Frederick, King of Prussia. The king one day rang a bell to summon his page, and not receiving an answer he opened the door and found his page fast asleep in a chair.

He advanced towards him, and was about to waken him, when the king perceived a letter hanging out of the page's pocket.

Curiosity prompted the king to know what it contained; so he took it out and read it. It was a letter from the young man's mother, in which she thanked him for having sent her part of his money to relieve her misery, and telling him that God would reward him for his filial affection.

The King, after reading it, went softly to his chamber, took out a purse full of money, and slipped it, along with the letter, into the page's pocket. Returning to his chamber, he rang the bell so loudly that it awoke the page, who instantly made his appearance.

"You have had a good sleep," said the King.

The page was at a loss how to excuse himself, and putting his hand into his pocket by chance, to his utter astonishment, found there the purse. He took it out, and turned pale when he saw what it was.

"What is that?" said the King; "what is the matter?"

"Oh, sire," said the young man, throwing himself on his knees, "some one is trying to ruin me. I know nothing of this money that I have just found in my pocket, nor do I know how it has been put there."

"My young friend," said the King, "God often does great things for us even in our sleep. Send that to your mother, greet her on my part, and assure her that I will take care of both her and you."

Children, filial love springs from the depth of the heart. A child that loves its parents sincerely rejoices when they are happy, and is sad when they are grief-stricken. What a beautiful example of tender love is that given to you, dear children, by the young Tobias. He could not be induced by Raguel, his father-in-law, to stay a few days longer after the wedding. "I know," said he, "that my father and mother now count the days; and their spirit is grievously afflicted within them." And to Raphael he said: "Thou knowest that my father numbereth the days, and if I stay one day more, his soul will be afflicted." Would to God I could say of all children that they love their parents with the same tenderness.

My dear children, a sincere love demands that you should rejoice the heart of your parents, by leading a virtuous life and praying for them. Nothing rejoices the heart of a good father and a pious mother more than the well-regulated, Christian life of their children. Parents value their children more than gold, silver, or precious stones; their eyes rest upon them with pleasure and satisfaction, and frequently in the joy of their heart they lift up their eyes to God, saying: "Thanks be to God! we have good and well-behaved children, who never cause us any sorrow."

Blessed Sebastian was a very obedient child. He never required to be told anything a second time, because it was his delight to attend to the first wish and to the first word of his parents.

One day he was left by his mother in the kitchen to watch some food which was boiling on the fire; he attended as faithfully as he could to the orders he had received, but, in spite of all his care, it boiled over, and was spilt upon the floor.

The little boy was very much troubled at what had happened, for, in a poor family like his, this was a great misfortune, and he knew how grieved his mother would feel at the loss. But he never thought of concealing what had happened, or even of making excuse as most children do. He almost expected that he might be punished, yet, when his mother came in, he went towards her, saying at once: "O mother, if you like, I am ready to be beaten, because the pot on the fire has all boiled over."

His mother did not punish nor even scold her little son, because she was a good woman, who rejoiced to see this proof of Sebastian's truthfulness and obedience.

If you love your parents sincerely, you will pray for them always; when they are stricken down by sickness do not fail to send for the priest. Should you lose your dear parents by death, let it not be said of you: "Out of sight, out of mind." St. Louis, King of France, when in Palestine, received the news of his mother's death; at once he retired to pray for the repose of her soul. Then he had many masses said for her, and sent stipends to the various churches of his dominions, that prayers might be offered for the soul of his dearly-beloved mother.

Such was the solicitude of this holy son. And if you follow his example by loving your parents sincerely it will be well with you here and hereafter.

FIRST SUNDAY AFTER EPIPHANY
Respect to Parents

"And he went down with them, and came to Nazareth, and was subject to them."

In these few words, my dear children, the evangelist sums up eighteen years of the life of our Lord and Saviour, Jesus Christ. "He was subject to them." To whom? To Mary, His mother, and to Joseph, His foster-father. Therefore, the Child Jesus is a most perfect pattern for each and every one of you, to show you how to fulfill your duties towards your parents. If you reverence them, if you love and obey them, you render them that honor that God requires at your hands. And why should you not love them with all the ardor of your heart? Do they not represent God as your Creator, because it is through them that the Almighty called you into life? And are they not your preservers, in that they take His place in looking after the health of your body and the good of your soul?

It is related of the Blessed Thomas More that he never left his home, even in the days of his power, without having first asked on his knees the blessing of his aged father. What an admirable example for us! For Sir Thomas More was a man who had gained the plaudits of the world,—a man whom princes and kings sought as an honored friend. Yet we see him, unspoiled by the flattery of a nation, caring only for the benediction of that aged one whom he called by the loving name of father.

I once heard of two sons who bore a very great love to their widowed mother. As this good woman did not have the use of her limbs, it was impossible for her to hear Mass on Sundays. Of all her afflictions, this seemed the hardest to bear, for she was a devoted adorer of the Most Holy Sacrament of the Altar. Her sons, knowing the anguish she suffered, determined on a plan by which they could satisfy her pious wish. To her old armchair they attached two poles, and by this means they were able to carry her to God's temple. The people of the village where they lived, seeing them approaching, gathered flowers to strew in their way, and begged God to shower His blessings upon them. Soon the news was brought to the pastor of the church. Ascending the pulpit, he chose for his text: "Honor thy father and thy mother, as the Lord thy God hath commanded thee," and his sermon was full of force, for his people felt that in the two noble boys they had an example worthy of imitation. So will it be with us, if we honor those whom God has placed over us.

A touching incident that happened in the life of Pope Benedict XI. ought to teach us the reverence we should pay our parents, no matter in what condition of life they are placed. This good man was the son of an humble shepherd. When he was raised to the Pontifical Throne, and word being spread throughout Rome that his mother was coming to visit him, the whole city went out to do her honor. Magnificently dressed, she was introduced into the presence of the Pope. Disappointed, the Holy Pontiff turned away with the words: "That lady cannot be my mother for she is too poor to purchase such a costume." Not a word would he speak to her while she was so attired, but when she returned later wearing the humble gown he knew so well, he lovingly embraced her saying: "Ah, this is my mother now! There is no one in the world that loves his mother more than I do mine."

Again, my dear children, let me impress upon you that you ought to be very obedient to your parents, doing all that they command,

and avoiding all that they forbid. By your good behaviour give joy to those that take God's place in your regard, and above all, be ready to extend to them a helping hand in their poverty and old age.

There was once an industrious cabinet maker, who seemed to be amassing not a little wealth. One day, a neighbor asked him what he did with all his money. He replied: "With part I pay my debts, while I put the rest out on interest." The other asked him to explain what he meant. He answered with a smile: "I mean just what I say. I give back to my aged parents the money they have spent on me—that is my debt—and what I now spend on my children, I look upon as capital which I hope to get repaid with interest when I am old." Are not the words of this man but too true? What our parents do for us is a debt which we are bound at some time of our lives to repay.

No more examples are needed, my dear children, to show that it is a sacred duty for you to honor your parents throughout your whole life. To the Fourth Commandment alone does God attach a temporal blessing, for the words of Holy Writ respecting it are: "Honor thy father and thy mother that thou mayest be long lived upon the land which the Lord thy God will give thee." Yes, honor them always, my children, and God will reward you by restoring you to their embrace when the shadows of this life have passed away.

SECOND SUNDAY AFTER EPIPHANY

Marriage With God and Without God

"There was a marriage in Cana of Galilee, and the mother of Jesus was there. And Jesus also was invited, and His disciples."

One thought from the text of to-day that ought to leave its impress on your minds, my dear children, is that the Mother of Jesus, and Jesus Himself, were guests at this humble wedding. It is remarkable, indeed, that nowhere in the holy Gospels do we find it recorded that our Divine Saviour attended a wedding of the rich, yet here "in Cana of Galilee" He is present at a marriage of the poor. How very happy must not this bride and groom have felt to be honored with His Sacred Presence!

And why did the Redeemer of the world interrupt His mission, as it were, to attend this humble ceremony? To teach us that thereby marriage was raised to the dignity of a Sacrament, and that only such a marriage, where Jesus and Mary are found in the hearts of the bride and groom, is worthy of His divine blessing. At Cana of Galilee, it is certain that only good people, pious and simple souls, were present, else our Divine Lord and the Blessed Virgin would not have been there.

From all this we may learn how full of consolation to Holy Mother Church is a Catholic marriage—a union where man and wife profess the same faith, and, side by side, receive the same Sacraments.

On the contrary, how unsatisfactory and full of evil forebodings is a mixed marriage—a union between a Catholic and a non-Catholic. Divided on the main point, religion, husband and wife are constantly at variance. The one cannot understand the views of the other, and so religion is a subject that must not be discussed, for if it is, a quarrel is sure to ensue.

On a bright sunshiny day, some years ago, a Catholic young woman and a Protestant young man were united in the Sacrament of Matrimony. Things went on smoothly for some months, but as time passed, the Catholic wife found that her religion was becoming the subject of constant quarrel. In fact, if she wished to attend Mass on Sunday, it meant she would have to endure for the rest of the week the cruelty of her tyrannical husband. Silently she bore his bodily injuries, thinking that her patience at least might have an effect on him. But no!

One day, all too soon, the end came. Her husband had come home for dinner, and finding the meat not to his liking, he was silent for a few moments, but the expression of his face showed how far his evil passion had gained the mastery over him. Suddenly he darted towards her, clenching his knife in his hand and with fury and rage flashing from his eyes. The poor wife turned deathly pale, and swooned away in fright. Some time after she regained consciousness, but not for long, for in a day or two she died, unmourned by the man to whom she had pledged her life.

This, my dear children, is but one case out of many, showing the sad consequences of a mixed marriage. Is it any wonder the Church forbids us to enter into such unions? At times, it is true, they may lead to the conversion of the non-Catholic party, but, as a rule, they have not the blessing of Almighty God.

Another beautiful thought, my dear children, is suggested to us in to-day's Gospel. "And the wine failing, the Mother of Jesus said to Him: 'They have no wine.'" How tender is the consideration of the Mother of God for the feelings of the young bride and groom. "They will be mortified if they realize that their guests are without due provision," the Blessed Mother thinks within herself, and turning to Jesus, she explains their need. Just a simple request, yet Jesus, on account of it, works His first miracle before His time. How tenderly does Mary thus teach us the lesson—if we want anything we must ask for it. Let us lift up our hearts to God in prayer, when we are in need. In His own good time He will hear us, if we only persevere long enough.

There was once a heathen boy who had been stolen by soldiers from his father's home, and taken to a distant country. There, Catholic missionaries were preaching the gospel to the natives, and among those to receive the gift of faith, was the stolen child. At his baptism he was given the name of Thomas. As he was devoted to his parents, and longed to be with them again, his constant prayer was that the good God would some day lead them to the country where he was. One day, the priest of the settlement, seeing the youthful Thomas gazing with longing eyes over the sea, said to him: "Thomas, my child, what are you looking at so earnestly?" "I am looking to see if Jesus has heard my prayer," replied the boy. "I asked Him to send my parents here that they might become Christians, and I want to see if the ship is coming."

Day after day, for two long years, Thomas went down to the shore,—one thought uppermost in his mind—"Would God hear his prayer?" But day after day he returned, disappointed. Still, he never wearied. No word of distrust escaped his lips. He was constant and hopeful, where others would have faltered.

At length, after long waiting, the priest, one day, saw the boy running towards him, his face wreathed in smiles. "Well, Thomas," said the venerable man, "what makes you so happy?" "Oh, Father!" cried the boy, "Jesus has heard my prayers at last. I knew He would! My father and mother have come. They are in the big ship that has just landed."

And so would our prayers be answered, my dear children, if our faith were anything like that of the little Thomas.

Let us pray then perseveringly when we are in any necessity. Even if a miracle is needed, Jesus will work that miracle at the entreaty of an humble prayer. And let us not forget to ask the Mother of God to intercede for us with her Divine Son, for He cannot do otherwise but grant her petitions now, just as he did in the days of old. Above all, may Jesus be always in our company whether at work or at play. Recreation and enjoyment are necessary for us, after we have done our due share of work. Why then should we not ask Jesus to bless it too, so that we may gain merit for heaven?

THIRD SUNDAY AFTER EPIPHANY

Sin, the Leprosy of the Soul

My dear children: How beautifully the Church places before our eyes to-day, the compassionate and tender mercy of our Divine Lord! Two men in dire affliction have only to name their requests, and their petitions are granted. The first sufferer, a leper, meets Jesus as He comes down from the mountain, and having adored the Man-God, begs in pleading tones: "Lord, if thou wilt, thou canst make me clean." And forthwith our Lord touched him, saying: "I will, be thou made clean."

In our Lord's time, my dear children, the fatal disease of leprosy had made great headway. No matter what precautions were taken, the people did not seem to be able to stay its progress. Those afflicted with it were obliged to remain outside the city walls for fear of spreading the dread contagion. Nowadays, such persons are exiled to Molokai, an island of the Hawaiian group, where charitable priests and religious devote their lives to the cause of aiding these poor unfortunates. In our Lord's day, however, there was no such charity exercised in their behalf. Their nearest relatives shunned them,—their lonely desolate lives were pitiable in the extreme.

But of what is this disease of leprosy a type, my dear children? Of sin,—mortal sin. On every side of us to-day there are lepers spreading their foul contagion far and wide. We do not notice them, for they are subject to no civil laws. They are not kept without the city gates; they mingle with us daily,—yet they are covered with a leprosy of the soul, far more fatal than the leprosy of the body. They are hideous in God's sight, and should be so in ours. And we too may become one of them if we do not avoid mortal sin.

The great St. Philip Neri loved God so much that he thought of nothing else all day long; and his whole life was spent in trying to induce others to love God also. He used to say: "Oh! if I could only keep people from offending God, how happy I would be!"

On one occasion, a number of boys were amusing themselves in the room where St. Philip was reading. As their noise was almost unbearable, some one complained of them to the saint, but he quietly answered: "Let them alone; let them play. There is only one thing I wish, and that is, that they keep from sin."

My children, that is the only evil we should dread in this world —sin. Yet we must not despair. If we have been so unfortunate as to fall from grace, the Sacrament of Penance is always at our command to restore us to God's friendship. Our good Jesus did not send the leper away, disappointed in his hope; neither will He fail us, if we come to Him, desiring to be cured. As St. Augustine says, God cures all evils, but only for those who ask Him to do so.

Yet, although by the Sacrament of Penance we are cleansed from sin, we must always remember that we are still most unworthy of God's grace. "Lord, I am not worthy," said the centurion, and this word the Church teaches each one of us to repeat, especially when we are preparing for Holy Communion. Many seem not to receive the Blessed Sacrament of the Altar with the proper dispositions! They show it by their exterior conduct, and by their indifferent and heedless bearing, when approaching the altar rails.

In childhood, my dear children, you should accustom yourselves to receive our dear Lord frequently, so that you may never be afflicted with the leprosy of the soul. Your hearts should be pure and holy, full of humility, reverence and love. When the time comes for Holy Communion, you should call upon the angels and saints to accompany you to the Holy Table, and to help you receive your God devoutly.

It is related that a pious nun once had a vision during Mass, at the time when the people were kneeling to receive Holy Communion. As the priest descended from the altar, she saw Jesus in visible form in the Sacred Host. While the holy man was distributing the sacred particles, Jesus seemed to stretch out His arms and to be most eager to unite Himself to some of the communicants, but to show signs of disgust as He approached others. On seeing this, the nun lovingly said to Jesus: "My dear Lord, why do you approach these so unwillingly since they seem to be as devout as the others?" Jesus deigned to reply: "My daughter, the souls into whom you see Me enter so gladly are those who always try to please Me; the others are full of faults and sins."

Once more, my dear children, let me urge you, when you go up to the altar of God to receive Him in the Sacrament of His love, do it with all the fervor in your power. Ask our good Mother Mary to prepare your little heart to be a fit abiding place for her Son, that each Communion may lead you nearer to the Throne of God, there to praise and bless Him forever and ever.

FOURTH SUNDAY AFTER EPIPHANY

The Most Precious Gift—Our Immortal Soul

My Dear Children:—Can you imagine a storm at sea? If you have never been far out on the deep blue ocean, with only God's heaven overhead and the restless billows beneath your feet, you cannot draw a picture in your minds of the sublime awfulness of a storm on the deep. But there is something akin to it—something that all of you know and have witnessed, and that is—a storm on land. How the wind roars, the lightning flashes, the thunder peals! Everyone hurries to a place of safety. And you, my children, how you seek mother and father for their protection,—as if anyone could shield you when the elements are raging. Far, far more dreadful, though, is a storm at sea. Away from every human aid, the ship is left to battle with the waves, or sink beneath the deep. But why should we speak of a storm at sea? Why call to mind a scene where God alone can offer succor? Because, my dear children, we are all sailing on the sea of life, where storms arise but too frequently,—storms that can be quelled only by the Most High when we cry to Him in our distress: "Lord, save us, we perish."

A ship going out from port is laden with rich treasures of merchandise. So, too, your souls, my children, after they have been washed by the waters of Baptism, are laden with treasures—graces which God heaps upon you from the very beginning of your existence,—graces that make the just soul a thousand times more precious than all the treasures of earth.

St. Catherine of Sienna, often favored by God with holy visions, was one day shown the beauty of a soul in the state of sanctifying grace. So fair was it to look upon, that its brightness dazzled her. "O my God!" she exclaimed, "if I did not know that there is only one God, I should think that this soul were one."

The Blessed Raymond, her confessor, asked her to describe to him as far as she was able, the beauty of the soul she had seen, but she answered, "My Father, I know nothing in the whole world that could give you the least idea of it." How beauteous, therefore, my children, must the just soul be!

Should a storm come at sea, how careful is the captain of the ship, and how vigilant the officers and sailors! They do not spare themselves until the danger is over. With the same diligence must we guide our souls, for, by day or night the devil may raise a storm of temptation around us that will surely engulf our frail barques, if we are not ever watchful. Our Lord Himself urges us, "Watch and pray lest ye enter into temptation." We must ever have a field glass in our hands to discern in the distance the faint outlines of rising storms.

A young man, anxious to please God and save his soul, asked his mother one day to tell him how he could easily overcome temptation; "for," he said, "I am very frequently tempted to do wrong." Without reply, his mother left him for a moment, but soon returned bearing in her hand a ring. With a tender smile, she said, "Take this ring, my child, and wear it always." To his surprise the young man noticed engraved upon it the words: "Watch and pray." "Every morning and night, and whenever you are tempted," his mother continued, "look at this ring and recall to mind the words you see engraved upon it." Obedient to his mother's injunction, the young man slipped the ring on his finger, and ever afterwards took care to follow her advice. His difficulty in resisting temptation speedily vanished, for his watchword had become—"Watch and pray."

Men at sea, my dear children, make use of certain signals to denote an approaching storm. So must we employ certain signs—prayer, fasting, the sign of the Cross, and love of Jesus, that the tempests of life may not vanquish us.

During the long career of Sister Grace of Valencie, who died at the age of one hundred and twelve years, Satan did not cease to tempt her. As she was fully aware of her weakness, she always turned to Jesus for help, made the sign of the Cross, and in consequence was ever victorious. Her implicit trust in God and her use of the Holy Name of Jesus, proved effectual means of banishing the demon.

Guided by a skilful pilot, a ship, no matter how far the journey, is sure to enter the harbor in safety. But who is the skilful pilot on your ship of life, dear children? It is your confessor who knows the dangers that threaten you and how to avoid them. If you follow his instructions, fulfill his commands, and abide by his precepts, the safety of your voyage is already assured. You will see in the far distance the eternal shore where some day, God grant, each little soul before me now will furl its sails, never more to wander from the haven of rest, secured for us by Jesus Christ, our Lord.

SEPTUAGESIMA SUNDAY

Working Out Our Salvation

Have you ever noticed, my dear children, how frequently our Blessed Lord mentions farmers in his discourses to His chosen people? He seems to have a particular liking for the tillers of the soil, and well He may, for God, who sees the hearts of men, knows that they, by their very avocation and mode of life, are free from many of the vices that threaten the lives of those who are residents of the metropolis.

In to-day's Gospel there is presented to our minds a husbandman who has care of a large vineyard. And he "went out early in the morning to hire laborers," "and having agreed with the laborers for a penny a day, he sent them into his vineyard."

Now, my children, who is this husbandman, so anxious to have good workmen for the culture of his soil? None other than God Himself. And the vineyard is your own dear soul for the welfare of which He has hired you to labor, that when the day of this short life is past, He may give you your wages—the glories of Paradise. From your earliest childhood, God has placed this vineyard in your care. The question now remains to be answered: Have you worked hard? Have you labored as God wished you to labor? Or have you not rather spent your days in idleness, caring little about the concerns of your immortal soul? Review briefly the actions of your life since you reached the use of reason,—and what verdict must you pass upon your conduct? Your thoughts have been mainly directed towards the enjoyment of the world's pleasures; your deeds have been performed out of mere self-love; your whole life, perhaps, has been an idle, useless one, devoid of God and of His holy teaching.

Of the bright little faces of the boys here gathered around me, I know some would answer to the name of Martin,—but do those boys know anything about their patron Saint? Well, St. Martin was a heathen child with no idea of the good holy God. One day, however, he went into a Christian church, and what he saw and heard there made him renounce the heathen practices and become a Christian. At the early age of twelve, he wished to leave his home to be a hermit in the desert, but, as his father had been an officer in the emperor's army, the young boy, when fifteen years old, was obliged to take a military oath, thus binding his life to the service of his country.

So holy and pure a life did he continue to lead, nevertheless, that, though his fellow-soldiers were astonished, they loved him for his goodness. His exceeding pity for the poor was also remarkable, for he bestowed his money freely on those whom he knew to be in need.

One bitter winter day, as he was riding on horseback, he met a poor man shivering with cold and almost naked. Full of pity and compassion, Martin immediately took off his rich cloak and cut it in two, giving half to the poor man. But our dear Lord would not be outdone in generosity, for, that very night, Jesus appeared to the soldier in a vision and returned him the half cloak he had bestowed in charity.

After eighty years of service devoted to God, St. Martin died, leaving behind him a marvellous example of how a soldier's life, despite its manifold dangers and temptations, may be entirely pure and holy.

SEPTUAGESIMA SUNDAY

Hour after hour, my dear children, our Blessed Lord knocks at the door of your heart, renewing His call for admittance. Oh! do not close it against Him, but rather beg Him to come in, and remain forever with you. Every little opportunity that God gives you to do something for Him, is a call to your heart alone. What if He has to go away disappointed?

The Saints did not treat our Blessed Lord as you do. St. Rose of Lima was particularly anxious to do everything to please Him, and never to allow His knock to go unanswered. As a little child, she bravely repressed her tears when her thumb had to be amputated on account of an injury. In pain of any kind, she always thought of our suffering Saviour, Who had submitted to far greater torments for her sake. She fasted three times a week on bread and water, and on other days she allowed herself only vegetables. Being compelled to listen to many flattering speeches on account of her rare beauty, Rose, to avoid all this, cut off her hair, and disfigured her soft skin by rubbing pepper on it. As a maid in the Gonzalves household, she worked day and night without interrupting her communion with God. On her head she wore a wreath of flowers with thorns turned inward, so as to resemble our Saviour in His acute sufferings, and no matter what pain she had to endure, she never ceased to pray and to perform works of charity and penance.

If you look over the history of the Church, my dear children, you will find that, just as the husbandman in to-day's Gospel hired laborers at different hours of the day, so God calls souls to work in His vineyard at different periods of their lives. Many are called in youth, many in manhood, and not a few at the very end of life. Yet all who have served Him faithfully in the time allotted to them, shall receive the same reward—the joys of Heaven.

The great St. Paul was born of Jewish parents and studied in Jerusalem. While still a young man, he held the clothes of those who stoned St. Stephen, and in his burning zeal to kill every disciple of Christ, he journeyed, on one occasion, to Damascus. But near this city, a light from heaven struck him to the earth, and he heard a voice saying, "Why persecutest thou me?" Before him he saw the form of Him Who had been crucified, and in tender accents, so unlike his infuriated threats of old, he cried out, "Lord, what wilt Thou have me to do?" St. Paul arose from the ground another man—a new creature in Jesus Christ. Thus was the persecutor of the disciples of the Man-God called to work in His vineyard.

Is not this good God worthy to be served from your very childhood, my dear little ones? You have each and every one of you been nurtured in the Catholic Church, and, therefore, it has been your privilege to have been called at the first hour by our Blessed Lord. See to it that when the evening of your life comes and the Master is paying each man his hire, you, too, may receive the promised reward—the Kingdom of Heaven for all eternity.

SEXAGESIMA SUNDAY

The Word of God

My Dear Children:—To-day our Blessed Lord takes us by the hand and leads us far out from the city's bustle and turmoil, into the peaceful country. As we walk along an unfrequented road, we see in the distance a large field in which a sower is planting seed. And as he sows, passing up and down the long furrows, some is falling by the wayside, and some among thorns and briers, but most of it falls on the good ground that the farmer has tilled.

Then we hear our Blessed Lord telling us that the seed is the Word of God, sown by the Divine Husbandman in the field of our hearts. If we listen to that Word and endeavor by all the means in our power to make it fruitful, our soul is the fertile soil that is spoken of in the Gospel.

Once a Jesuit Father was sent to one of the Western States to do some missionary work. In a letter to his superior he wrote the following: "In my missions there are two little boys who have given me great consolation and edification. Though the miserable hut in which they live is seven miles away from the church, these two boys have come every day for six months, to hear me explain the Catechism. One very cold, wet morning, having gone as usual to the chapel, I found my little lads already there, but trembling with cold. Putting my hands on their heads, and looking into their sturdy little faces, I whispered: 'You might have remained at home to-day, boys. It is so bitter cold.' But they answered that they couldn't afford to miss one instruction, as they wanted to learn more about God." What fine little characters to have around, my children, and what grand men they must have one day become!

Holy Scripture says: "He that is of God heareth the word of God,"—so, my dear boys and girls, never give the excuse if you stay away from sermons: "I do not need them. I know all the priest has to say." People who never go to Mass, and habitually transgress the laws of God and His Church, speak in that strain. And, anyway, if you knew every doctrine of the Church a thousand times over, that would be no reason why you should neglect hearing the Word of God.

A monk one day thus addressed his superior: "What is the use of my going to hear sermons? I can never recall what has been said." In order to convince him that he always gained some benefit from what he heard, the superior commanded him to take one of two baskets and bring him water from the river. The monk was much surprised, but nevertheless he obeyed without a murmur. Three times the command was repeated, and three times the holy man returned with the basket as empty as before. Then the superior asked him what difference he detected between the basket he had tried to fill with water and the one that had been left untouched. "None," replied the monk, "except that the one I carried to the river looks cleaner than the other." "Just so," answered the superior; "as the basket, despite the fact that it could not retain the water, became cleaner, so your soul, though perhaps unable to retain all the instruction you have received, yet derives some benefit from every sermon."

Do not imitate those people, my children, who never give themselves time to hear the word of God, but who have more than enough leisure to parade the streets, and to be anywhere and everywhere save in the house of God. St. Bernard warns us that there is no surer sign of eternal damnation than to despise God's holy word.

There dwelt in one of the cities in which St. Peter Alcantara was preaching, a lady of high rank, conspicuous for her great fortune and vanity. Having heard much of St. Peter's holy life, and the many conversions he effected by his preaching, she felt a strong desire to see him and listen to one of his discourses. Accordingly, one day, magnificently dressed, she went to the church where the Saint was preaching. She took a position near the pulpit, so that no word of his might be lost. As she raised her eyes to the man of God before her, she was filled with amazement, for she beheld one whose body was emaciated and worn out by austerities. Immediately she contrasted her own vain life with his penitential one. With the deepest attention she listened to his words, after which she returned silently to her dwelling. From that moment she began a new life. Restless and sick at heart, she hastened to the house where St. Peter resided, and in deep humility threw herself at his feet. Having made a good confession, she changed her prodigality into abundant alms, and applied herself to prayer and mortification, in the exercise of which virtues she persevered fervently till the hour of her happy death.

Dear children, be not you among the number of those who neglect to hear God's word. If you listen to it with reverence, it will be the means of making known to you His holy will; it will encourage you in temptation, support you in trial, and make you increase in virtue. What a great consolation it will be to you at the hour of death if you have listened to it attentively during life, and observed it faithfully till time for you has passed away.

QUINQUAGESIMA SUNDAY

Miserable Condition of the Sinner

My Dear Children:—Of the many afflictions to which we poor human beings are subject, none is so great as blindness. The loss of hearing, of speech, or of the power of our limbs, may be compensated in some way or other, but to be totally blind is a condition of life from which even the most courageous of us would shrink in terror. Think of it, my dear children! If we could not see the beauty of the heavens on a starlit night, nor watch the vivid play of the lightning in the storm-driven clouds,—we could not see the return of the violet, the daisy or the buttercup in our meadows,—nor could we follow with our eyes the variegated plumage of the birds, winging their flight through our woodlands. No,—all would be total blackness! Sight, then, is surely the greatest faculty we possess.

And so we can appreciate, at least in a small degree, the condition of the poor blind man on the road to Jericho. But of whom is this blind man a type, my dear children? He is a type of the sinner, who, careless of his soul's welfare, gives full sway to his passions and leads an unmortified life. What blindness do these poor souls display! They exchange the friendship of God for a perishable treasure; they barter their eternal salvation for a moment's sinful joy!

A little girl whose name was Agnes had just reached her fifth birthday,—and in honor of it her parents had invited their friends to dine with them. Agnes's god-father, on meeting her, slipped into her hand a gold-piece as a birthday gift. The child, of course, was overjoyed when she realized that the money was her very own, and no one could induce her to part with it. Soon, however, the little girl, wearying of the length of the dinner, ran outside to amuse herself. Just at that moment a woman was passing by, carrying a basket of fruit. The child still hugging her treasure, ran towards her and cried out: "Look! Just look what I have! It's a beautiful piece of money." The woman, seeing the coin, answered: "Yes, it is inded very beautiful. But see! here is an apple, larger and more beautiful than your money. However, if you will give me the coin, I will give you the apple." Joyfully the child made the exchange, thinking that thereby she was the gainer. After the woman had received the money and hurried away, Agnes ran into the house, to show the apple to her mother. On being asked where she got it, she quickly made answer, "A good woman who was passing by gave it to me in exchange for my money." At this Agnes's mother was justly provoked and was about to scold the child severely, when the god-father interposed: "What is the use of scolding the little one? Didn't she think that the apple was of greater value than the piece of money? Let her alone. She will understand, by-and-by."

Yes, my dear children, Agnes surely learned her mistake as she grew older, but isn't it strange that no matter how old some people are they never understand that the endless joys of heaven are not to be exchanged for the fleeting pleasures of the world?

When we are blinded by sin we are unable to see our own ruin and destruction. There are examples of this occurring every day, but we need only look at one of them to realize how ruinous to the soul is this spiritual blindness.

A miser who begrudged himself the very necessaries of life was on one occasion taken seriously ill. The doctor, thinking that the patient could live no longer than three days, advised him to send for the priest and make his peace with God. This advice, however, the miser refused to follow. Instead, dragging himself out of bed, he searched for his banknotes, and threw a roll of them into the fire, for fear anyone else might enjoy his money when he was gone. The next day the doctor called again, only to find his patient much better. After some time, the miser did recover, but as he had burned up almost all his money, he soon had to beg his bread from door to door. How blind did not the sin of avarice make this man, my children! How much better would it not have been for him if he had given some of his money to the poor, so as to secure for himself treasure in heaven!

Another grave cause of spiritual blindness is dangerous reading. The reader of bad books and papers not only arouses sinful thoughts within himself, but also causes his mind to hunger after more of such literature.

A priest once gave to a man condemned to death a book which he read both with profit and pleasure: "Ah!" exclaimed the man, "if I only had had books like this to read, I would not be where I am now."

We are told that at the age of twelve St. Teresa lost her excellent mother, and that about the same time the child fell into the dangerous habit of reading love tales and romances, in which she was encouraged by a young cousin who had come upon a visit to her father's house. Every day the youthful Teresa gave a greater portion of her time to the reading of this dangerous literature, and the consequence was that she soon became idle, worldly, and vain of dress. No doubt she might even have fallen deeper had not her father placed her in a convent of Augustinian nuns, where, removed from the occasion of sin, she again recovered her former virtue.

Like the blind man of Jericho, my dear children, we should constantly cry out: "Lord, that I may see." We must recognize our spiritual blindness and beg God to remove it if we wish to gain His friendship. Like the blind man, too, we must have confidence in our Divine Lord, believing firmly that He has the power to lighten our afflictions and heal our wounds.

As a reward of this confidence the day will come when the shadows will disappear, and our blindness being removed, we shall see, in all its beauty, the vision of our God forevermore!

FIRST SUNDAY IN LENT

ON MORTIFICATION

For the last three Sundays, my dear children, you have noticed that the priests of God's Church were robed in purple—the color of penance—and yet it is only on Ash Wednesday that Lent really begins. Why, then, does the Church, as early as Septuagesima Sunday, remind us of the season of penance by the purple vestments of her ministers? Because the first Christians, being far more fervent than we are, began their fast three weeks sooner. They imposed rigorous penances on themselves, they fasted strictly, they practised the most severe self-denial, and yet it was not because they had sinned more grievously than we, but because they loved God more. Let us then try to learn during these forty days the lesson of mortification they have so zealously taught us.

Now, the Church, being a kind and gentle mother, does not oblige you, my dear children, to fast. You are growing and need food to give you strength. Still, there are many little acts of mortification you can perform in order to prepare yourself worthily for the great feast of Easter. It is perhaps very hard for you to arise the moment father or mother calls you. Instead of murmuring, say to yourself: "I must get up immediately for the love of Jesus. It is He that is calling me, and will I refuse to answer?" Or perhaps you have what is known as a "sweet tooth." Cakes and candies are always pleasing to you. Here is another chance, then, of practising self-denial. Promise Jesus that you are going to make a sacrifice of these dainties during Lent. And, suppose your way from school lies past a church. Oh! what a golden opportunity. Tell our Lord that you are going to visit Him more frequently in the Sacrament of His love; *you* are going to keep Him company if all the world neglects Him. With such sentiments as these you will assuredly spend a holy and happy Lenten season.

Of all the Saints, the humble St. Zita gives us an admirable example of mortification. She rose early in the morning, recited her prayers devoutly, and attended Holy Mass. At meals she was satisfied with a little. In fact, she fasted rigorously most of her life, and did many other works of penance. Though she suffered much from her mistress and fellow servants (for she herself was only a poor working-girl), still she overlooked their cruel treatment of her and repaid their insults by doing acts of kindness for them. All her sufferings she united with those of our Divine Lord, and no matter what humiliations she had to endure, she never changed the sweet tone of her voice nor forgot her gentle, quiet ways. And why should we not imitate St. Zita in her wonderful self-denial? There are so many opportunities of being kind to those whom we dislike—so many priceless chances of showing our love to God a little more than we have ever done heretofore.

Another brilliant example of mortification is the good St. Anthony. At twenty-one he left his home to spend the rest of his life in the desert. There his only food was a little dry bread with salt, while his only drink was water. And he indulged in this but once a day—after sunset. Satan often came in visible form to tempt this good holy man. Now the archfiend would frighten him by making a loud noise; again he would vent his rage upon him by striking him until he was almost half dead.

In the discourses which St. Anthony gave to the disciples whom he had trained to live as he himself was living, he often said, "Believe me, my brethren, Satan is more afraid of the fasting, prayers, mortifications and good works of the servants of God than of anything else they do, because by these holy exercises they inflame their hearts with God's fire of love."

If the body will not obey the law of God, my children, severe means must be tried to bring it into submission. By the works of penance which the saints of all ages have performed, we are taught the lesson, how to subjugate our body. We must not give it everything it craves; and not only will the observance of this rule make us masters of the sensual appetites, but it will also be a means of prolonging our lives. Unless we mortify the flesh, it will become unmanageable; it will gradually lead us to commit the most grievous sins, and in the end bring us eternal damnation.

As I mentioned before, my dear children, the Church, on account of your tender age, does not require a strict fast of you, but all of you are obliged to abstain from eating meat on Fridays throughout the year. Unfortunately there are many Catholics who carelessly transgress this law and thereby give grave scandal. But be you, my children, most exact in observing it during your whole lives. The very care you take not to eat meat on forbidden days is in itself a fast.

King Stanislaus of Poland was always a faithful observer of the ancient discipline of the Church. In Lent he ate but one meal a day, not even allowing himself a collation in the evening. On Fridays he denied himself the use of fish and eggs. From Holy Thursday noon till the following Saturday noon, he did not take any nourishment, not even bread and water. That interval, consecrated to our Lord's Passion, he devoted, as far as his affairs permitted, to prayer and almsgiving. Yet, notwithstanding these austerities, this good king lived to the grand old age of eighty-four years. Can mortification, then, be said to shorten life? And if a king has practised such exceptional self-denial, cannot we do something, too? Or are we always to be the laggards loitering in the rear?

Oh! let it not be said of us, my children, that we, the favored ones of God's house, are hard-hearted enough to behold our Lord Jesus Christ suffering and dying for us, and not do anything in return. Let us learn to love and practise mortification. Should the evil spirit come to us, even in the guise of an angel of light, let us not believe his lying protestations. No; let us rather say to ourselves: "I have resolved to serve another master—my good God, my Redeemer; and Him only will I adore!"

SECOND SUNDAY IN LENT

Heaven

To-day I am going to tell you, my dear children, of the most beautiful thing God has made. Have you ever witnessed from the crest of a mountain the sun rising amid the golden-hued splendors of the morn? Or watched the same sun slowly descending 'neath the silvery gate of evening? Have you ever seen the pale moon shedding her beams of effulgent brightness on a foaming sea? Or, on a clear, calm night viewed the star-bedecked heavens, like so many precious jewels gleaming from an open casket? If you have ever watched God, the Master Artist, changing the scenery of the heavens, then you must have exclaimed in sheer amazement: "Oh! how beautiful! Could God make anything more glorious, more worthy of our admiration than this?" Well may you ponder the magnificence of the earth and sea and sky, my children, yet you should not stop here; God *has* made something far more beautiful than human eye has ever seen, and that masterpiece is—Heaven.

In the town of Ranban, in Cochin-China, there lived, not many years ago, an eminent physician who was at the same time a fervent Christian. His greatest joy was to convert his pagan countrymen, and though most zealous in healing their bodily infirmities, he never neglected their spiritual wants. One of the missionary fathers gives an account of a vision of heaven which this good holy man once experienced. The father writes: "Not long after my arrival in that province the doctor was attacked by a dangerous illness, so dangerous, indeed, that his life was despaired of. The people to whom he had endeared himself, hearing of his condition, immediately gathered around his bedside to pray for him. They were already reciting the prayers of the dying when suddenly some one noticed that he had ceased to breathe. To their utter surprise, however, he came to and said: "Oh! I have seen wonderful things—I have seen heaven!" "Tell us," they said, "what God has shown you." "That is impossible," he murmured, "for no tongue can describe, no mind can conceive the wonders I have seen." Then he was silent. A few moments afterwards he added, "I saw many in heaven whom I knew here on earth as models of piety for their brethren." As a proof that it was not a mere dream but a real vision, he immediately rose from his bed, free from all sickness. From that time on till his holy death, he lived an examplary life, using the concerns of this world merely as a means to an eternal end."

Why was our Blessed Lord transfigured before the eyes of the Apostles on Mount Tabor, if not to teach us that divine favors are reserved for those who by their virtues raise themselves above the trifling employments of earth? Let us correspond then with the desires of our Redeemer. Everlasting glory is promised only to those who take up their cross and persevere in His holy service. Heaven is to be won only by tribulation and suffering.

It is related that Charles the Fifth, King of France, once placing on a table in his room his crown and sceptre, and on another his naked sword, called his son into his presence and said to him: "My son, make your choice between this table and that." Taking up the sword without a moment's hesitation, the young boy replied with a smile: "I choose this, because with it I can win the sceptre and crown."

So it is with the Christian, my dear children. By success in the warfare of life, the crown is won; by bearing courageously the sufferings of earth, the glories of Heaven become our reward.

"And Peter answering, said to Jesus, 'Lord, it is good for us to be here: if Thou wilt, let us make here three tabernacles, one for Thee, and one for Moses, and one for Elias.'" How entranced St. Peter must have been at the Transfiguration of our Blessed Lord, since he desired to remain on that bleak mountain forever! Oh, my children, if a single ray of the glory of Christ could cause such profound emotions in the heart of St. Peter, what will our transcending joy be when, at the resurrection, we shall rise immortal, and shall behold our God in the splendor of His majesty!

Will you then for a momentary pleasure renounce the everlasting delights of Heaven? No, my children, I cannot believe that you will. Rather I feel that you will do all in your power to fight bravely the battles of life that the crown of victory may be forever yours. Remember that the grace of the good God shall not be wanting to you.

And what is it that our dear Lord requires of you? O, so much less than He required of the martyrs and saints! He desires you to persevere in the practises of your childhood, to be faithful to your prayers, and zealous in the worthy reception of the Sacraments. He asks you to curb your passions, to resign your will entirely to His holy guidance. Could He ask less? Let this be your daily resolution, my dear children: Cost what it may, I will do all in my power to be true to the ideal God had in His Divine mind when He created me,—I will do all in my power not to lose the place He has destined for me in the Kingdom of Heaven.

THIRD SUNDAY IN LENT

Sin of Envy

My dear Children: One quality that seems particularly to characterize our Blessed Lord throughout His most holy life is His infinite compassion for poor weak human beings, the creatures of His hand. "He had compassion on the multitude." This word, again and again, sums up His attitude towards the miseries of mankind. On His trips through Judea and the surrounding country, we find Him invariably followed by the blind, the deaf, and the dumb, and these poor sufferers never sought Him in vain. Just as sure as they presented their sick bodies to His healing touch, they were cured of their afflictions. And so in to-day's Gospel we see our Divine Lord work a prodigious miracle: "Jesus was casting out a devil, and the same was dumb." Now, how did the onlookers regard this stupendous action that was taking place before their very eyes? If we read the inspired words a little further, we will glean that "the multitude were in admiration at it; but some of them said, 'He casteth out devils by Beelzebub, the prince of devils.'" Herein we see, my children, that though the miracles and examplary life of our Lord gave Him a great following,—though everybody was anxious to see and hear Him,—and though the multitude gathered around Him,—still some looked askance at His miracles, and put false constructions on His charitable works. These were the evil-minded Pharisees who would neither enter Heaven themselves, nor permit others to enter.

But, my dear boys and girls, the Pharisees of our Lord's time have many followers even at the present day. There is a class of people who pass the most unfavorable judgment on the most saintly works, saying anything and everything in their thoughtlessness. If one goes to Holy Communion regularly, they call him a hypocrite; if one is good and kind, they term him a sneaky character; in short, a bad boy or girl can see absolutely nothing good in a well-behaved, religious child. Such virtue is foreign to their nature, and consequently they cannot understand how it can exist in other hearts. Immediately they become jealous,—envious of those who are leading a better life than they,—and rash and untrue judgments are the result. Guard against the vice of envy, then, my children, particularly with regard to the good qualities of your companions. It is an abominable trait of character, hateful both to God and man.

St Genevieve, it is said, while still very young, fasted and prayed, not only for a few hours at a time, but even for weeks and months. Soon her holy life began to be known far and wide, and people marvelled how one so young could do so much for God. Satan's wrath being aroused against the saint, he put it into the minds of those who had been her friends to say that she was a hypocrite,—a pretender. The very people who once praised her now turned against her, and this became to the young saint one of the heaviest of her crosses. A good pious man, St. Germanus, seing the malice hidden in these reports, and being enlightened by the Holy Ghost, knew that envy was the cause of the evil. "No," he said, "what you say of that child is not true, for she is as holy in her inmost soul as she appears to be in the eyes of the world." Thus was the young girl freed from the censure of malicious tongues.

Another point to be considered in to-day's Gospel is the actual miracle performed by our Divine Lord—the restoring of speech to the dumb man. Have you ever asked yourselves, my dear children, why God has given you a tongue? Is it not to pray, to sing His praises, to speak the truth, to confess your faults, to comfort the afflicted? Is it not to use that tongue entirely for His honor and glory? But as much good as the tongue can do, so much evil also can it accomplish, for it is a world of iniquity, as St. James says. How many do not purchase for themselves eternal ruin by their malicious sins of the tongue!

A dumb woman was one day brought to St. Vincent that he might confer on her the gift of speech. Although she had never uttered a word before, she said to the Saint: "Give me the power to speak, and direct me how to lead a holy life." To her appealing petition St. Vincent calmly replied: "You may be directed how to lead a holy life, but as to the power of speech, it is better for you to be dumb than to be damned for the sins of the tongue. Even though you now speak, that power shall forthwith be taken away from you." No sooner had the saint uttered these words than the woman became dumb as before.

"From the abundance of the heart the mouth speaketh," our Blessed Lord Himself has told us; therefore, if God be in your heart, He will also be on your lips. In this one thing at least we can all imitate the saints: we can keep vigilant watch over our tongues so as never to utter an uncharitable word, never to tell a lie nor speak about our neighbor's faults. By such sins we abuse the faculty of speech which God has conferred upon us.

St. Francis de Sales was so straightforward as a boy that he never tried to palliate his faults in any way by excusing himself. It happened one day that he broke a glass by accident, but he preferred to be punished severely rather than say the least thing contrary to truth. His good mother had so instructed him: "Never tell a lie, my child. Lying lips are an inheritance from the devil, and, therefore, a child that tells a lie is a child of Satan." These words made such an impression upon the youthful Francis that he preferred the severest chastisement rather than utter a falsehood.

Learn this lesson, my dear children, from the Gospel of to-day: Never be envious, for thus you will avoid many unjust judgments and sins of the tongue. None of you wish to be like the Pharisees who went with Jesus on His journey from place to place. Rather be ye among the faithful disciples who would follow Him even to prison and to death, because you believe that He is Christ, **the Son of the living God.**

FOURTH SUNDAY IN LENT

Holy Communion

What gentle, persuasive eloquence our Divine Lord must have used, my dear children, to induce these good people of Judea, sometimes even for days at a time, to leave their ordinary avocations and hie with him to mountain or desert in order that they might receive the doctrine of truth falling from His sacred lips! They were so eager to hear His words that the Evangelist tells us they even forgot to partake of food. But Jesus knew that they were hungry, and that was enough. Accordingly he performed another stupendous miracle,—the multiplication of the loaves.

All you children hearing my words know what it is to be hungry. As soon as you have said your prayers in the morning, the first thing you ask is, "Mother, is breakfast ready?" And when you come home from school, too, you like to visit the pantry to see if there are any goodies around. Now if I asked you, my children, "Why do you eat?" you would immediately answer, "If we did not eat, Father, we could not live." And it is a similar response our Lord uses when the question applies to our immortal soul. Just as the body needs food to keep it alive, so the soul needs sustenance to save it from eternal death. And what is the food that Jesus has given us and left here amongst us till the end of time? None other than Himself in the Holy Eucharist, the Blessed Sacrament of the Altar. Every day, from the rising of the sun till the going down thereof, this mystical bread is multiplied and distributed in His name.

To the great edification of all his subjects, Henry IV., King of France, was a frequent recipient of the holy Sacraments. He was thus ever prepared for death. "You know," he used to say, "I cannot foresee what is going to happen to me, and I want to be always ready to die." It was fortunate for him that he thus kept himself in the state of grace, for one day he was attacked by an assassin and cruelly murdered. In speaking of him St. Francis said, "The greatest happiness of this good king was to be a dutiful son of the Church, and it is this thought that now gives me consolation. He was well prepared, and I am confident that God has been gracious to him."

Like this pious king, my dear children, you should ever keep yourselves prepared for death. You know not what may befall you. It behooves you then to be on your guard, so that when our Lord gives the final summons you may be ready to respond to His gracious call.

With what ardent delight must not the good people, for whom our Lord worked the miracle of the multiplication of the loaves, have partaken of the repast furnished them by the Saviour of the world! In like manner, should not the soul of the worthy communicant experience a heavenly joy when receiving the sacred Body of our Blessed Lord?

It is related by Father Hunolt, of the Society of Jesus, that two students once agreed that, if God would allow it, the one who should die first should appear to the other and tell him how he fared in the next world. Shortly afterward one of them died, and, by permission of God, appearing resplendent with heavenly glory to his fellow student, he told him that through God's mercy he had been saved. The other, congratulating him on his happiness, asked him how it was he had merited such favor from Almighty God; to which the happy soul replied: "I have merited it by the care with which I always tried to receive Holy Communion worthily." With these words the spirit disappeared, while his companion experienced feelings of the deepest consolation, accompanied by an ardent desire to imitate His example.

If our Divine Lord sees you, my dear children, approach the Holy Table with true affection, He will return you love for love and become for you a support in all your trials. When you go to Holy Communion, therefore, you should give evidence by your exterior conduct of the deep interior recollection that fills your soul. Always approach the altar with reverence and holy fear, lest the sacred Bread of which you partake should serve to your condemnation rather than to your sanctification.

Not many years ago, a little girl, devout and pure as an angel, knelt at the altar-rail on a certain Sunday, and earnestly begged her Saviour, whom she had just received with sentiments of tender devotion and glowing love, to let her die before she would soil the white garment of her innocence. And behold what happened! In the evening, a little after sunset, her pure soul took its flight to heaven. Her parents laid her out in the same white dress she had worn in the morning, and, though many tears were shed over her coffin, still the bitterness of the mourners was assuaged by the consoling thought that God had called the child in her innocence, whilst, if she had lived, she might not have saved her soul. Her father, who for many years had been a slave to his passions, was so touched by the death of his child that he renounced his evil life and was thoroughly converted.

The Holy Eucharist sustains our soul in the wilderness of this world, and enables us to reach the true mount of God. Let us then, my children, often partake of this heavenly nourishment, so that we may one day enter into the kingdom of celestial glory, there to praise God in everlasting happiness forever and ever!

PASSION SUNDAY

Sin and Its Consequences

"They took up stones therefore to cast at Him: but Jesus hid Himself and went out of the temple."

To such lengths as this, my dear children, did the hatred of the Jews for our Divine Lord carry them in their frenzy: "They took up stones to cast at Him." Those who had received only benefits from that sacred Hand, those who had been healed of divers diseases by its Divine touch, now turn their backs upon their benefactor and wish to kill Him. Can such hatred enter into the mind of man against man? Even of man against God? Ah! It is only too true, my dear boys and girls. And the Jews are not alone in their sin of base ingratitude. Do not you, too, show your hatred against your greatest benefactor,—God, your supreme Good,—when you commit sin? And what means it to have the Almighty as your enemy? You remember the terrible sentence passed against Lucifer when he revolted against his Maker: Powerful as he was before his fall, he, the most resplendent of the heavenly intelligences, was hurled to the depths of hell. Oh, what a fearful thing it is to fall into the hands of the living God! And if man in his poor finite nature rebels against his Creator,—when the measure of his iniquity is complete,—he, too, is cast into the dread abyss. Remember the words of our Blessed Lord: "Fear not them who can kill the body, but rather fear the one who can cast both body and soul into hell!"

Two soldiers were one day passing through a town where a

mission was in progress. They had but little religion and both were leading sinful lives,—but one of them said to his comrade: "Let us go to hear a sermon." No sooner said than done. They entered the church and found the good missionary preaching on hell.

When the sermon was over, they rose and left the church together. Having reached the street the one said to the other: "Do you believe all that the priest said?" "No," responded his companion with a satirical laugh; "I believe it is all nonsense,—sheer nonsense invented to frighten people." "Well, for my part," rejoined the first speaker, "I believe it; and to prove to you that I am sincere, I intend to quit the army and repair to a monastery." "Go where you please," said the other; "I shall continue my journey." And so the two parted.

His journey was not yet completed, however, when the last speaker fell ill and died. His companion, now in the monastery, hearing of his death, prayed thus to God: "O my God, reveal to me the state of the soul of my friend who has just departed." For his greater good God was pleased to let his companion appear to him. Recognizing him at once, the monk asked, "Tell me, where are you in the next world?" "I am in hell," replied the other in direful accents; "I am lost for all eternity." "O wretched man," responded the monk, "and do you now believe what the missionary said about that place of torments?" "Yes, I believe it," he groaned. "The missionary was wrong in only one thing: he did not tell us the hundredth part of what is suffered here." Having spoken these words the apparition disappeared, leaving the penitent soldier thanking God for the grace he had received.

By sin, my children, you sell yourselves to the devil; you become his slave; and Satan, in wrathful jealousy lest you may reach heaven, deprives your soul of all its merits, and thus takes away its rights to eternal reward. The good actions you have performed, the Masses you have heard, the Holy Communions you have received,—all, all are of no avail if you die in mortal sin, and stand before your Maker poor and forsaken, with no one to help you. By mortal sin you renounce your heirship to heaven. Just as a man who would destroy all his furniture, set fire to his home, and throw his money into the river, would be regarded as a madman, so you too are utterly devoid of sense if you barter your eternal welfare for sinful joy by committing even one mortal sin.

A strange story is told of a certain man who in pagan times was condemned to suffer a fearful punishment for some crime he had committed. His sentence was that a dead body should be fastened to him in such a way that he could never loosen himself from it. The wretched man trembled with fright when he saw the terrible load he was to carry, and when he felt its weight pressing upon him, the feeling of his close companionship with death pierced his very bones. In the light of day, he constantly discerned the eyes of the dead man turned upon him; in the darkness of night, he suffered the intolerable anguish of realizing that the putrid body was his only companion. At last, the poor wretch lost his reason, and died from the effect of his terrible punishment.

Children, this is a fitting picture of the sinner who goes about day after day, weighed down by the crimes that are bearing him onward to destruction. Therefore, my dear boys and girls, if you are in sin, resolve to go to confession that you may cleanse your soul from every stain. Let nothing estrange you from your God. Wherever you are, model your life on the purity and innocence of our Lord Jesus Christ and His Blessed Mother, that they may receive you at your death into the eternal mansions.

PALM SUNDAY

Preparation for Holy Communion

"And a very great multitude spread their garments in the way; and others cut boughs from the trees, and strewed them in the way; and the multitudes that went before, and that followed, cried, saying: 'Hosanna to the son of David; blessed is He that cometh in the name of the Lord.'"

How different is the attitude of the people towards our Divine Lord as recorded in this Sunday's Gospel, compared with their sentiments on the occasion when "They took up stones to cast at Him." To-day we see the Redeemer of the world royally welcomed by His chosen people. They hail his coming with joy; they chant a glad "Hosanna to the son of David," while some even spread their garments in His way to do Him honor.

And do we ever realize, my dear children, that the very same Jesus who was received to-day by the inhabitants of Jerusalem with acclamations of joy, comes into our hearts so frequently in Holy Communion? Oh, what a grand reception we ought to give our regal guest. How ardently we ought to try to cleanse our hearts from all sin, especially from mortal sin! How pure and holy should be the soul that wishes to receive its Lord God devoutly! How unspotted the heart into which the Author of Purity so often enters! Therefore, my children, throughout your whole life endeavor to make most careful preparation for Holy Communion, that you may never receive our Divine Lord unworthily in the Sacrament of His Love.

Years ago, it is said that a young man, addicted to bad habits, had nevertheless resolved to make his Easter Communion. Scarcely had he received the Blessed Sacrament, however, when he was possessed by the devil. The Bishop of the diocese, having ascertained the reality of the possession, sent a priest to exorcize the demon. "Now answer me," said the minister of God to satan, "why didst thou take possession of this unhappy Christian?" "Because," replied the demon, "I have a right to him. He is mine since he made a bad Communion." This declaration struck such a salutary fear into the minds of the bystanders that they resolved that they would prepare themselves more worthily in the future for the reception of the Blessed Sacrament of the Altar.

God vouchsafes to give us occasionally such an example as this, my children, that we may never commit the sacrilege of receiving Him unworthily.

Alphonsus, King of Aragon, whose piety outshone his wisdom, on one occasion went to visit a nobleman of his kingdom, shortly before the feast of Easter. The latter, although very wealthy, entirely neglected his religion and gave himself up to a sinful life. On hearing that his king was coming to visit him, he made great preparations to receive him royally.

Alphonsus, pleased with the marks of respect shown him, turned to his host as he was about to leave, and said: "Most noble Lord, you have given me a magnificent reception, for which I am deeply grateful, but I ask you now, on the coming feast of Easter, to give a welcome to a nobler King than I, your Lord and Saviour, Jesus Christ. Prepare your heart to receive Him worthily."

Profiting by his sovereign's advice, the nobleman, to the edification of all, received Holy Communion worthily the following Sunday.

Not only must our hearts be adorned with virtues, my dear boys and girls, when we would approach our Lord in the Blessed Sacrament, but we must also have ardent faith in the Real Presence. That little host, so white, so pure, lying there on the altar, after the minister of God has pronounced over it the sacred words of consecration, becomes truly and really the body of our Lord Jesus Christ. Our senses may deceive us, our faith never!

Once, in the palace of Louis, King of France, Mass was being celebrated, when, at the words of consecration, our Lord, under the form of a beautiful child, appeared visibly on the altar. Immediately word was brought to the king that he might come and witness the miracle. But Louis gently answered: "I firmly believe already that Christ is truly present in the Holy Eucharist. He has said it, and that is enough. I do not wish to lose the merit of my faith." And he did not go to see the wonder.

Do all that lies in your power, my children, to receive our blessed Lord most worthily on the grand feast of Easter. Each Communion for which you have lovingly prepared your heart will make you a little better, cause you to resemble Jesus a little more, and give you a greater desire to be united to Him for all eternity.

EASTER SUNDAY

The State of Grace

Gloom and sadness, my children, shrouded the Christian world during the last few days—gloom and sadness caused by the death of our Lord and Saviour Jesus Christ: "Greater love than this no man hath than that he lay down his life for his friend." And this is what He, the Son of the Omnipotent God, has done for us. Yea, to prison and to death He was led, of His own free will, to atone for our many sins. But to-day the note of sadness is forgotten, for "this is the day that the Lord hath made. Let us be glad and rejoice therein." All over the world, from shore to shore, the peal of the organ, stilled during Christ's sorrowful Passion, is heard reverberating. All over the world the glad tidings are re-echoed: "The Lord is risen indeed and hath appeared to Peter." How well does not this picture typify the Christian! His dark and gloomy hours are those that he spends in sin; his glorious, happy moments, those that he passes in the company of Jesus risen from the tomb. No wonder that after the penitent sinner has tasted the delights of companionship with the Son of God, he breaks with the old careless life and pledges anew a sacred allegiance to his Maker.

In a town of Italy, many years ago, was born a woman who is known in the Church of God as Blessed Angela. The offspring of a noble family, she for a long time led a careless life, regardless of her duties to God, till one day she received from that Divine Hand the grace of returning to the path of rectitude.

She herself thus speaks of her condition: "For some time I

suffered in my soul a strange feeling which gave me no rest. The greatness of my sins, together with the thought of the severe punishment awaiting me, was constantly before my mind. One thing above all inspired a salutary fear in my breast—the consideration that I could never obtain pardon for my sins without going to Confession. Ashamed as I was to reveal all my wrong-doings, I chose to cloak my guilt by making a bad confession. I even went further and hesitated not to receive unworthily the Blessed Sacrament of the Altar. Time went on, yet with no surrender to grace on my part. Rather the confession of my sins grew more difficult, but my conscience gave me no peace. Most earnestly did I pray to God to send me a confessor, who would help me in my pressing need. One day I met a religious on his way to preach a sermon in the church I attended. I accompanied him, and when his discourse was ended, I begged him to hear my confession. There and then I told everything that I had done in my whole life. It is needless to add that I arose from my knees renewed in spirit and thoroughly happy. I thanked God for His boundless mercy to me in bringing me back to Him, and out of gratitude I imposed on myself most severe penances."

My children, Blessed Angela is now among the saints of God. So shall we also be, if, imitating her repentance and perseverance, we arise from the grave of sin to the life of grace. And yet it is most difficult to do this, for the devil makes tremendous efforts to retain in his power those whom he has once entrapped by his evil seductions. Far better is it for us to preserve our baptismal innocence, so that we may never become his prey.

It is related that a miller, a hardened sinner, once refused to make a mission which was going on in his town. However, at the earnest solicitations of his relatives and friends he finally consented to go to Confession. So great was the crowd surrounding the confessionals that he had to wait for three or four hours before his opportunity came. Just as he was about to kneel at the side of the priest, a cry of "Fire! Fire! The mill is on fire!" resounded through the church. He heard the cry; he knew all it would mean to him if he lost everything; yet with the thought, "I must free my conscience now," he calmly knelt down before the minister of God and confessed his sins with sentiments of profound sorrow. On his way home he learned that it was another man's mill that had burned, and not his own.

See, my children, how the evil spirit hated to lose this man's soul. Had he left the church in answer to the cry of "Fire!" it is possible that the grace of conversion might not have been given him again. But he responded to God's call and thus freed his soul from the tyranny of the evil one.

As Christ began a new glorious life after His resurrection, so also must we, on arising from the grave of sin, enter upon a life entirely different from the old. The frivolities and vain things of the world must be discarded if we would live with Christ. In trials, in sufferings, in death itself, we should encourage ourselves by the words of St. Felicitas: "Look up to heaven, my soul. There Jesus Christ with His saints awaits you. Fear not passing sufferings, but rather fear the tortures of eternal punishment!"

FIRST SUNDAY AFTER EASTER

God Alone Gives True Peace

Those first sad days after our Blessed Lord's ignominious death, my dear children, were trying ones indeed for the Apostles, and though with the Easter dawn the shadows were dispelled, still "for fear of the Jews," as the Gospel tells us, the followers of Jesus kept themselves secluded in that upper chamber in Jerusalem. And "when it was late that same day, the first of the week, and the doors were shut where the disciples were gathered together for fear of the Jews, Jesus came and stood in the midst, and said to them, 'Peace be to you.'" What loving words, "Peace be to you!" Why did our Lord choose to couch His meaning in this simple wish, rather than discourse with His disciples in eloquent persuasive language? Because, my dear children, the greatest gift God can bestow on us here on earth is peace. It matters not how poor we are—if peace is our dowry we are content; it matters not how much of the world's goods we possess—if peace is wanting we are in misery. Our hearts were made for God, the Author of Peace, and they will be restless till they rest in Him.

While hunting one day, a prince named Josaphat lost his way in a deep forest. Suddenly he heard some one at a distance singing very sweetly. Surprised to hear such a lovely voice in the depths of the thicket, he directed his horse to the spot; but his astonishment when he found there a poor leper can better be imagined than described.

"Alas! my friend," said the prince, "how can you in your dreadful condition have the courage to sing?"

"My lord," replied the leper, "I have every reason to rejoice. For forty years I have lived in this world—my soul confined in the dark prison of this body. Now the walls of the prison are falling to pieces, and my soul, filled with heavenly peace, will soon take its flight to God. Why should I not be overjoyed at this thought and sing praises to my Creator for all His benefits to me?"

The soul of this poor leper, my dear children, must have been overflowing with that peace which surpasseth all understanding. He had learned to value worldly concerns at their true price; he realized that nothing is lasting but God alone. And you, too, my children, though now life is full of promise and allurement for you, though you may think that the riches of the world promote happiness, still a day will come when all things will appear to you in their true light, when you shall realize that only by loving God alone you can possess true peace. Avoid all sin, my children, for it begets nothing but misery. The days of innocence are always happy and contented ones. While you remain holy and pure, no bitterness fills your heart, no disquiet affects your mind. But if satan is once allowed dominion over your soul, then peace and happiness take wing.

Do you know what a great emperor once said? Congratulations were being showered on him from every side, for he had just won a world-famous victory. When asked if he did not deem that day the happiest of his life, he quietly answered, "No, the happiest day of my life was the day of my first Holy Communion." That was the verdict of a man who had enjoyed all the honor and glory of the world, a man who had strayed from the path of innocence he had trod as a child, and yet, see how he disdains all earthly fame and names his first Communion day as his day of crowning happiness and joy.

What heavenly delights did you not also experience, my children, on the day when you received our Lord into your heart for the first time! What unalloyed happiness is not still yours when you approach the Communion rail with a pure, clean heart! Oh! never turn your back on our blessed Lord in the Holy Eucharist! If you are true to Him, He shall never forsake you, but shall be your support both in life and in death.

All that I have said so far is to teach you, my dear boys and girls, the necessity of being at peace with God and ourselves. However, we must also be at peace with our neighbor and do all in our power to preserve peace amongst others.

St. Francis de Sales, in Rome on a visit, once hired a room for himself in a house on the banks of the Tiber. One evening on his return to his lodging, he found his servant engaged in a dispute with the proprietor about his room. The condition of affairs was, that, as a party of strangers had just arrived, the landlord needed an extra apartment. Immediately St. Francis interposed: "I will have no quarreling on my account," and turning to his servant, he added: "Come with me. We will take up our abode somewhere else."

It happened that an exceedingly heavy rainfall on that very night caused the river to overflow its banks to such an extent that many of the houses along the river front were washed away, and the inmates drowned. Among these was the house in which St. Francis had previously lodged. It is safe to attribute the saint's miraculous preservation to his peace-loving disposition.

Do you remember, my dear children, the Eight Beatitudes given by our Lord in His Sermon on the Mount? One was, "Blessed are the peacemakers, for they shall be called the children of God." Now, if you want to be numbered among God's special clients, it is your duty to preserve peace among your little companions. Children of a peaceable disposition are loved and admired by everybody. They are never engaged in quarrels, for they would rather relinquish their own ideas than become involved in dissensions of any kind.

There was once a rich man who daily provided bread for the children of the poor families in his vicinity. A large basket was filled with loaves, and each child was permitted to take one. But often the children quarreled among themselves as to who should take the largest loaf. In all these disputes it was noticed that one little girl took no part. Rather she was invariably satisfied with the last and smallest loaf in the basket. The rich man, being informed of the child's conduct, ordered several coins to be placed in the smallest loaf, which next day fell to her lot, as usual. Thinking it a mistake, the little girl took back the money to her benefactor, but he said: "Keep the coins, my child. I had them put in the loaf to reward you for your peace-loving disposition."

God does the same, my children. He gives peacemakers a hundredfold more than what they lose for the sake of avoiding dissensions. Let us then try to live in peace with God, our neighbor and ourselves. We shall have peace with God if we keep away from sin; with our neighbor, if we love him with a genuine charity; with ourselves, if we exert all our energies to accomplish God's holy will.

SECOND SUNDAY AFTER EASTER

The Good Shepherd of the Soul

My dear Children: By no better comparison could our Divine Lord have pictured His relations with each individual soul than by styling Himself the "Good Shepherd." The flock that has no shepherd goes astray and is lost, and so would we wander from the right path if God did not again and again act the Good Shepherd to our souls.

"I am the Good Shepherd." What a grand title, a title of love! "The Good Shepherd giveth His life for His sheep." So has our Lord given His life for us; nay, more, He has left that life, His own precious Body and Blood, to be the strength and the food of our souls. And why does He do all this? Out of pure love for us. God could have saved the world by the shedding of a single drop of His Blood! yet, look what He has done: "Wounds and bruises and swelling sores" were not too great a price to pay for our ransom. Death itself would be an easy sacrifice for the all-consuming fire of His love. And why does the Good Shepherd do so much for our soul? Why is it that He finds no rest till He has brought the poor erring heart back to Him? Because our Divine Lord, my children, knows better than all others the priceless value of a soul: A spirit immortal, made according to the image and likeness of God! Have we the faintest conception of the treasure we possess? Do we realize in the smallest degree the grandeur of our destiny? Look around you to-day and try to master the thought that it is the soul that calls into existence the masterprieces of the world. Painting, music, sculpture would not captivate our minds as they do, were it not for the soul of the artist behind them. As no one can see the mind itself, but can only point out the result of its workings, so no one can produce for us a graphic picture of the soul. How could they? It is a spirit invisible to our eyes—visible only in so far as we know of its action.

St. Augustine tells us of a certain doctor who doubted the existence of his soul, and in consequence believed that there was no future life—that all ended with death. One night he had a dream: A youth, standing before him in shining garments, questioned him, "Are you asleep or awake?" The doctor answered, "I am asleep." "Can you see me?" the youth continued. A decided "Yes" was the response. "How do you see me?" the visitor inquired, "do you see me with your eyes?" "No," replied the doctor, "I know not how I see you." "Do you hear me?" queried the young man, "do you hear me with your ears?" "Yes, I hear you," was the answer, "but not with my ears. I know not by what means I hear you." Thereupon the angel, for such the youth was, said to him: "The action of your senses is now suspended, yet you see, hear and speak. A time will come when you will not be able to use these senses of yours, yet seeing, hearing, and speaking will be as easy for you then as it is at the present moment." Then the angel disappeared and the doctor awoke, but from that day he firmly believed in the existence of a future life.

The soul has been created for God, my children, and for heavenly companionship with Him for all eternity. Therefore, it is our bounden duty to consider the saving of our soul as the most important business of our life.

Otto, Emperor of Germany, on one occasion while on his way to Rome, passed near the dwelling-place of a hermit named Nilus, known throughout the country for his holiness of life. The emperor having called on him, and having been treated courteously, said to him before leaving: "Nilus, ask of me what you wish, and I will joyfully give it to you." "All I ask," replied the saint, "is that you save your soul; for although you are an emperor, you, like other men, must die and be judged. Therefore, have a care for your eternal welfare." Otto withdrew, but he never forgot the hermit's good advice. Long years after, he died a holy death.

Even if you were the greatest kings and queens of the world, my children, possessing gold and silver and estates without limit, you would have to die, and of what use would all these things be to you if, gaining them, you lost your soul?

Long, long ago a man, by name Macedonius, one day heard a sermon on the words of our Lord: "What will it avail a man if he gain the whole world, and suffer the loss of his own soul?" Such a deep impression did the discourse make upon him that he immediately left his home and became a hermit to prepare for eternity. Many years afterwards it chanced that a king on a hunting trip in the forest suddenly came upon the place where the hermit lived. Surprised to see a human habitation, he entered and asked the saintly man what he was doing there. Macedonius, turning to the king, said: "And what has brought you here, my Lord?" "I came to hunt in the forest," was the answer. "That same reason brought me, too," replied Macedonius, "but I came not to hunt the poor animals, but to seek the eternal rewards of heaven." Then the king pursued his journey, reflecting deeply on the words of the holy hermit.

If you wish to save your souls, my children, you must toil and suffer much. Be generous with God, for the reward which the Good Shepherd has prepared is exceedingly great. Imitate St. Rose, who, amid all her sufferings and afflictions, never lost the sweet calm of her soul. Clinging to God in firm faith, she cried out, year after year, "Lord, increase my sufferings, and with them Thy love in my heart." The longed-for answer from the lips of Jesus at length came: "Rose of My Heart, be thou my spouse forever!"

THIRD SUNDAY AFTER EASTER

From Suffering to Joy

What sorrow must not have filled the hearts of the Apostles, my children, when they began to realize the meaning of Jesus' strange words: "A little while, and you shall not see Me; and again a little while, and you shall see Me; because I go to the Father." That Jesus, Who had been their support in trial, Who had conferred on them the power of miracles, Who had died on the Cross, and, though they had deserted Him, had met them on the same footing as before,—that Jesus was going to leave them,—He would be with them in bodily presence no longer! But this was not all that our Blessed Lord told His Apostles. He went on to say: "Amen, amen, I say to you, that you shall lament and weep, but the world shall rejoice; and you shall be made sorrowful, but your sorrow shall be turned into joy." If the disciples wished to prove themselves worthy of their Master, then they were to follow in His footsteps. As it was only by suffering and humiliation that Jesus attained His glory, so they could not reach heaven by any other path than the one He had trod. And so it is to-day, my children. Those who wish to follow Christ must be tried in the crucible of suffering. Sacrifice in one way or another is the teaching of faith; self-indulgence, the principle of the world. Choose your course: Do you wish to receive from Christ the rewards He promises to self-sacrifice? Or would you rather follow the maxims of the world and adopt its principle of self-gratification?

In the time of the Emperor Hadrian, St. Symphorosa and her

seven sons were brought before the dread tribunal to answer to the charge of being Christians. At first the emperor tried to gain the favor of the mother by flattering words—he promised the pleasures of the world to herself and family if she would renounce the foolish religious sect to which she belonged. But, skilfully uttered compliments and promises of worldly prosperity were alike unable to make an impression on that staunch heart. As a result, she was given over to the torturers. Her courage never failed under their barbarous treatment. She seemed immune to blows and stripes. Not even when she was suspended by the hair of her head did she utter a cry of pain. At last, she was drowned in the depths of the Tiber, and her seven sons, faithful to the precepts of their heroic mother, followed her to death.

Of what account was the wealth and honor offered by the Emperor Hadrian to St. Symphorosa, in comparison with the heavenly joys that awaited her? Oh, my children, the pleasures of this world are not worthy to be compared with the glory to come! Why should we then give way to a sinful momentary delight and thus risk our eternal welfare? The joy the sinner experiences lasts but a short while. Disappointment will follow; it *must* follow. Yet God is so good to us that He often afflicts us when we are in the midst of sinful enjoyment,—not to revenge Himself on us, but simply to make us return to Him.

St. Norbert, when already raised to the office of sub-deacon, lived a life of unrestrained pleasure. He even refused any higher orders in the Church, for fear his enjoyments would be curtailed. One day, bent on pleasure as usual, he started on horseback to a neighboring town. Overtaken by a terrible thunderstorm, he could find no refuge anywhere, so he was obliged to ride on. Suddenly a streak of lightning knocked him senseless to the ground. After a long time he regained consciousness, only to remember the purpose of his journey, and to feel that his sad plight was a punishment from Almighty God. With these thoughts in his mind, he cried out in the words of St. Paul: "Lord, what wilt thou have me to do?" To which a voice replied: "Turn away from evil and do good; seek after peace and pursue it."

This was the turning-point of Norbert's life. Forsaking all pleasures, he gave himself up to the practice of self-denial. Later, he became an archbishop and the founder of a strict religious order.

What will it profit you, my children, if you are rich in the world's goods, but poor in God's grace and friendship? What will it profit you to be gifted with the brightest intellect ever bestowed on a human being, if you surrender your brilliant faculties to the dominion of the devil? On the other hand, though you should be the poorest beggar walking the streets to-day, if you enjoy God's grace, you possess the needful essential for happiness.

Among the companions of St. Francis there was one, by name Brother Juniper, remarkable for his simplicity. No one ever saw him angry no matter what humiliations were heaped upon him. One day, passing along the street with St. Francis, he was accosted by a man who had been his companion in youth, but who now was irreligious and ungodly. With contempt he called Brother Juniper a fool for having left the world. As this appelation only made the good brother laugh, the man retaliated by every abusive word that came to his mind. Brother Juniper, still smiling, and taking up the ends of his cassock as though carrying something, said: "Come, —do not be so sparing with those precious stones. Throw me some more." So the good brother regarded the insults and injuries he met with as precious stones with which to purchase heaven.

A noble courage it is that a soldier shows, who keeps advancing in battle, even in the face of death. Far nobler, however, is the courage of the youth who proceeds ever onward in the battle of life,—onward in spite of the passions warring in his heart, and silently but strongly opposing his every step,—onward, in spite of the raillery and mockery of his companions, the allurements of pleasure, the applause of the world,—onward, in spite of the daily desertions that he witnesses in the ranks about him. Such a soldier on life's battlefield deserves the crown of glory which he shall assuredly win from the Hands of our Lord Jesus Christ Himself.

FOURTH SUNDAY AFTER EASTER

How to Serve God Cheerfully

The sad words spoken by our Lord to the Apostles, recorded in last Sunday's Gospel, my dear children, are repeated again to-day, and an additional thought is added: "It is expedient for you that I go, for if I go not, the Paraclete will not come to you." Much attached as the Apostles were to Jesus, it was only natural that when he told them of the coming separation, they were heartsore and distressed. Thereupon, He rebuked them for their sadness, but He offered no word of chiding for their deep affection.

This should be a lesson for us, my dear children. We should love our Divine Saviour with all the ardor of our hearts,—we should serve Him with all the earnestness of our love,—yet that love and service should never make us tend to sadness. "The Lord loveth a cheerful giver." Holy Scripture itself tells us "Rejoice in the Lord, and be not sad, for the joy of the Lord is our strength." It behooves us then to be bright and cheerful in God's service that thus we may lure other hearts also to give Him praise.

St. Macarius, a holy anchorite of the desert, sometimes left his cell to visit his brethren throughout the different parts of Egypt, that from their example he might learn to serve God with greater perfection. On one occasion, he and another brother happened to be crossing the Nile with two officers of the imperial army. The latter, attended by all the luxury befitting their state, descried at the other end of the boat the two holy men, shabbily attired but apparently exceedingly happy. Amazed at such content amid the direst poverty, one of the officers, going over to where they sat, said to them: "You appear to be happy although you seem to be very poor."

"You are right," they responded, "we *are* happy; but if we are made content by having forsaken the world's pleasures, how miserable must they be who live slaves to its enticements."

So strong an impression did these earnest words make on the officer that, as soon as he returned home, he discarded his rich garments, gave all he had to the poor, and, leaving the world, spent the rest of his days in prayer and solitude.

The greatest saints, my children, were always cheerful. St. Aloysius and St. Stanislaus, though very pious, never avoided the society of their fellow-students, but rather were eagerly sought by them. So ought you be—pleasant and cheerful to all your associates; no gloomy faces, no sad looks, just because you are trying to practise a little penance. Remember to serve God joyfully, for that is the kind of service He craves from His children.

In the first centuries of the Church, Peter, a Christian child, six years old, was awakened one morning to be told that he was to be beheaded that day with his father. Strong in grace, and eager to suffer for Christ, he expressed his joy at the good news, and, robing himself in his finest garments, he went forth, ready for the sacrifice. The headless body of his father met his gaze; but, undaunted by the sight, he calmly knelt down and prayed beside the corpse; then, loosening his collar, he presented his neck for the stroke. Soon his pure soul winged its flight to heaven.

If mere children have thus joyfully faced torture and death for the sake of Christ, how comes it that we look for sympathy in our small trials,—that we even begrudge the trifling penances we inflict on ourselves? Oh! let us be more generous in the future! Let us not give way to discontent and unhappiness because of our little sufferings. Let us rather ask God, with a joyful generous spirit, for greater trials to be borne for His love!

St. Pacificus, even as a little boy, often wondered why so many people devoted their lives so entirely to worldly affairs to the exclusion of heavenly interests. "How foolish they are!" he used to say. "They allow their hearts to cling to those temporal things which to-morrow perhaps they must leave forever!" When the devil tried to tempt him to sin by filling his mind with bad thoughts, the holy child drove away the tempter with the words: "Never will I do such a thing! Do you think I want to lose my cheerfulness of mind in this world, and lose heaven in the next? No, I will never place myself in that danger."

Like St. Pacificus, my dear children, we ought not surrender to the seductions of the devil. If we keep our hearts good and pure, there is no need of giving way to sadness. Let every one see by the cheery aspect of our countenances that we are God's own children, content to work joyfully for Him during our short day here,— content in the hope that we shall rest in the shadow of His Presence forevermore!

FIFTH SUNDAY AFTER EASTER

Prayer

My dear Children: How tenderly our good Lord exhorts His disciples to resort to prayer when in any pressing necessity! How lovingly He assures them: "Amen I say to you, if you ask the Father anything in My name, He will give it you." And are not we His disciples, His followers, my children, just as truly as if we were accompanying Him over the hills and valleys of Judea? If this is true, then why should we not also turn to the One who will prove our Comforter, our Sustainer, in all our difficulties?

If you want anything very badly, my children, do you not immediately go to father or mother with your request? And the experience of your young lives tells you that sometimes you have gained your desire, but often you have been refused. Your parents, who have your welfare so much at heart, sometimes answer your pleading tones with the words: "No, you cannot have what you wish. You do not need that now, my child. It would be harmful instead of beneficial to you." And perhaps you go away disheartened.

Our Lord occupies a similar place in our regard. He is our tender Father, to whom we turn in our afflictions,—and as His home is heaven, we must needs raise heart and mind to Him, addressing Him in that sweet communion we call prayer. And we must all pray, my children. Those who do not, run a great risk of losing their souls. God is only too willing to come to our assistance, if we ask Him in the right way.

Whilst on a journey one day, St. Ignatius and some of his companions hired a peasant to carry their baggage, as they were travelling on foot. He proved to be a very ignorant, impatient man, and the good priests often had to reprove him for the profane language he constantly used. Whenever the little party arrived at an inn, the fathers retired to a room and devoted themselves to prayer, while the peasant slept on a bench near the fire. However, noticing the happy faces of the holy priests as they prayed, the poor man began to think it was probably because of their fervor that they were so good and happy. So he determined to do as they did. It was not long before it was remarked that the peasant was giving up his evil habits one by one, and soon he was a changed man. See what the result of fervent prayer was, in this case, my children.

But you will say, "God knows our needs, why then must we ask for them?" Because a good father always likes his children to place implicit confidence in him,—to come to him for all their wants. In like manner, our Heavenly Father seeks the confidence of his creatures. If we turn to God with a holy, childlike simplicity, our prayers will surely be efficacious.

One morning, a poor widow said to her little ones: "My children, I haven't anything to give you to-day for breakfast. There isn't a loaf of bread in the house. Go and ask God in His mercy to help us." Disconsolate, and not knowing what to do in her distress, the poor mother prepared her little ones for school as usual. One boy immediately sought the church, and, entering, went up to the high altar. Not perceiving any one in the dimly lighted church, he began to pray aloud: "O good Father who art in Heaven, hear my prayer to-day. We poor children have nothing to eat. Send us something that we may not die." When he had finished his humble childlike petition, he went to school as his mother had directed him. On his return home, he was surprised to see a large loaf of bread on the table. "O mother," he cried joyfully, "God has heard my prayer." "Yes, in His own good way," replied the mother. "When you were kneeling at the foot of the altar this morning, there happened to be in the church a pious lady whom you did not see. She, hearing your prayer, was inspired by God to bring us these good things."

Prayer without devotion, my children, is displeasing to God and is of no avail, for He Himself once said: "These people honor Me with their lips but their heart is far from Me." Whenever St. Francis entered a church, he thus communed with himself: "Worldly and frivolous thoughts, stay at the door till I return again." Then he prayed as though he were alone on earth. In fact, his devotion is said to have been so great that he did not know what distraction meant.

My dear boys and girls, you know that if you want to enter a house that is locked, you must use a key, so if you desire to enter God's beautiful House—Heaven—you must use prayer, for prayer is the key of Heaven. Morning, noon, and night, do not neglect to pray. Above all, have recourse to God when you are beset by temptations. Finally, in the last critical moment of your life, turn your thoughts heavenward, and implore the sweet Virgin Mother that, as you have honored her Divine Son in life, so you may be united with her in singing His praises for all eternity.

SUNDAY WITHIN THE OCTAVE OF THE ASCENSION

THE SPIRIT OF TRUTH

According to our Lord's sacred words, my dear children, the Paraclete is the Spirit of Truth: "When the Paraclete cometh whom I will send from the Father, the Spirit of Truth who proceedeth from the Father, He shall give testimony of Me." As the Holy Ghost, then, was to be the Spirit of Truth for the Apostles, so He must be for us. We must love the truth, and avoid nothing more than the spirit of deception and lies. The Christian whose heart is the temple of the Holy Ghost should make that heart a fit abiding place for the Divinity, and this can be accomplished in no better way than by the avoidance of all falsehood. Yet, notwithstanding this, it is an unfortunate fact that many Christians allow the spirit of deception to creep into their very lives and become a part of their existence. Rich and poor, high and low alike, hesitate not to tell untruths, because they consider the evil of so little consequence. But have you not often heard Satan called the father of lies? Way back in the ages long since passed away, he began his wicked work—Adam and his posterity forfeited their right to the kingdom of heaven because he believed Satan's deceitful tongue. A liar, then, is simply a tool of the evil spirit, because such a one actually does the devil's work. And would you, my dear children, desire for one instant to be classed among the children of Satan? Then avoid the telling of lies, so hurtful to your own soul and to the souls of others. All the saints have detested even the first workings of deception.

There was once a young girl who, like many others of her age and sex, was so very fond of fine dresses that she hoarded her hard-earned money with this one ambition—to purchase costly wearing apparel. One day she bought for this purpose goods that cost her four dollars a yard. Her father on seeing the material and knowing nothing about its price, asked her the cost. Fearing a stern rebuke for such useless expenditure of money, the girl replied, "A dollar a yard."

Somewhat later, while the young girl was absent from home, a peddler came to the door offering his wares for sale. Seeing the fine material, he inquired what price had been paid for it, and on being informed "a dollar a yard," he immediately offered two dollars a yard for the whole piece. Considering that he was making an exceptional bargain for his daughter, the good father let the peddler have it without another word. When his daughter returned home he told her what he had done, adding that now she could purchase a far better dress for herself. But on hearing the words the girl, greatly troubled in conscience, revealed to her father all her previous deception. Angry with her for her falsehood, the father had no word of sympathy for her distress, as he regarded her punishment but too well deserved.

Even if the evil effects of lying did not exercise a baneful influence on the soul, my dear children, yet this vice ought to be avoided because of the shame and disgrace attendant upon it. No one will ever trust a person addicted to falsehood. His most upright actions will soon be called into question on account of the feeling of distrust with which he is regarded.

Not even in joke, my children, should a lie be uttered. Sometimes you are so desirous to play a trick on your companions that if you cannot gain your object by truth, you will not hesitate to tell a falsehood. Lies told in jest often become a more grievous matter than we are wont to consider them, or else bring about more serious results than we bargain for.

A man of a fun-loving disposition was once writing a letter at his desk, when his little daughter stole up beside him. The child, seeing ten bright gold coins lying near her father's hand, asked where they came from. With a little twinkle in his eye he replied: "Little one, don't you know those bright dollars grow on a bush called the gold bush? They are planted in the ground like beans, and the plant grows with dollars hanging on the branches."

It was only a simple joke that any older mind would not credit, but the child believed implicitly every word falling from the lips of her father. So while he continued writing, she quietly took the money, ran out into the garden, and buried it in the ground. Then she joyously returned to his side, saying: "You'll have a fine lot of dollars now, father. I planted every one."

In consternation the man sprang from his desk. "Come with me immediately, child," he said, "and show me where you put them." Vainly did the little one point out the spot; the gold was not to be found. Either she had forgotten the place, or else, someone, seeing her action, had removed it during her absence. This shows us, my dear children, what an unlooked-for consequence sometimes results from a lie told in jest.

Even by the heathens this vice was considered despicable. Among the Greeks all liars were branded so that others might avoid association with them. The Roman Emperor Claudius, too, considered liars an abomination. On one occasion, being informed that a Roman citizen who had recently died had been noted for his lying tongue, Claudius instantly ordered that this man's home should be destroyed and his family banished, so that all remembrance of him might be obliterated.

Consider, therefore, my children, how detestable lying is. God has given you a tongue to chant His praise, to solace your neighbor in sorrow, to utter no deceiving word,—and you perhaps use that tongue to tell untruths! Has it never occurred to you that that tongue which you employ to utter falsehoods has been touched time and again with the precious Body of your Lord, that He, your God, your All, has rested there when He came to you in Holy Communion?

Therefore, my children, always strive to be truthful, no matter what it may cost you, "nothing can need a lie." Then you, too, like the saints, shall ever advance in the way of holiness and truth!

PENTECOST

Courage for the Love of the Lord

My Dear Children:—Next to the tender, heart-touching feast of Christmas, and the majestic, glorious one of the Resurrection, the feast of to-day, when we celebrate the coming of the Holy Ghost upon the Apostles, stands paramount in the Church's calendar of God-given festivals. Our blessed Lord on various occasions during His sacred ministry had promised to send the Paraclete, the Holy Spirit, to teach His disciples all things and bring to their minds whatsoever He had said to them. Not only that, but this divinely-sent Spirit would strengthen their courage and fortitude in preaching the Gospel, and would induce in their hearts the acceptation of death amidst the most excruciating torments rather than part with their precious gift of faith.

But was the Holy Ghost to bestow only on the Apostles His inestimable blessings? Not at all, my children. He will grant both you and me the same favors to-day if we give Him entrance into our hearts. We, too, shall be blessed with the courage of the first Christians if we ask this Divine Spirit who "breatheth where He will" to come to us as He did to the Apostles of old.

At the time Father Fernandez was preaching the Gospel to a large crowd in a certain city of the Indies, a man approached the good priest as if to speak to him, but instead, spat in his face. Without saying a word in rebuke, the holy missionary took out his handkerchief, wiped his face, and continued his discourse as though nothing had happened. Filled with wonder at such saintly meekness, those who at first had joined in the vulgar laugh could not but admire the patience of the preacher. Among those present was a certain learned doctor, who, reflecting on what he had seen, said to himself: "Surely, this stranger's doctrine must be true and heavenly, for that which inspires such courage could only come from God." The sermon being concluded, the doctor publicly acknowledged that the preacher's virtue had convinced him of the truth of the Catholic religion. There and then he asked to be baptized. Thus was a soul saved, my dear children, through the meekness and fortitude bestowed by the Holy Ghost upon this good missionary.

Together with the numerous other gifts conferred on the Apostles by the Holy Spirit, was the gift of the love of God. Those who before the Crucifixion had deserted our Lord in His dire need, "They all leaving Him, fled," now burned with Divine love to go forth and inflame other hearts with the same holy fire. Yea, after the coming of the Holy Ghost tortures and death were considered by them cheap coin with which to purchase the kingdom of heaven. Such marvelous effects had the Third Person of the blessed Trinity wrought in their souls!

At Ozaca, it is related, there once lived two pagan boys, both under the age of twelve, who one day entering the church of the Christians and going up to the priest, thus addressed him: "Father, we desire to be baptized." Though the priest was fully convinced from their clear, definite answers to his questions that they knew well the principles of our holy faith, still he thought it advisable to make them wait a little longer because of the antagonism of their parents to everything Christian. But the boys would brook no delay. Throwing themselves on their knees before the holy man, they implored him to grant their petition, declaring, "Father, we refuse to stir from this spot till you baptize us." Unable to resist their importunity, the priest complied with their request.

Days passed, yet the parents knew nothing of their children's change of faith. Some time after, however, one of the boys, having bought a pious little picture, placed it in his bedroom. No sooner had the father seen it than he sent for his son and demanded: "Where did you get that picture?"

"It is the picture of a Christian saint, father," replied the boy.

"And what have you to do with such things? You are not a Christian!"

"Yes, father, I am," came the quick response.

"What!" exclaimed the enraged man, "you a Christian! If you do not instantly adore the idols, I will put you to death!"

"Father," answered the child, "you may do as you wish, but I will remain a Christian!"

Seizing the boy, his infuriated parent stripped off his clothes and cruelly beat him with leathern thongs, only taking time now and then to demand more savagely than before: "Are you still a Christian?" But the brave child could not be made turn traitor to his newly-found faith. Though the blood was now flowing from his many wounds, he still answered: "Yes, a Christian, and I will die such!" Very soon his poor body was mangled from head to foot, but he uttered no word of complaint. Even when the cruel father presented the child to the gaze of his pitiless family, and the only greeting he received was jeers and ridicule, he still remained steadfast and patient. By some chance, however, the governor of the province heard of the father's barbarous conduct, and sending for him, he reproached him publicly, declaring that henceforth the boy would be under the emperor's protection, since this father was incapable of exercising parental rights. Thus was this inhuman father deprived of his child.

The love for Christ and the strong courage of this mere boy, we too need, and need badly, my dear children. Let us then supplicate the Holy Spirit that He may enkindle in our hearts this fire of love, that, like the Apostles and saints of God, we may become strong in words and example and thus lead other souls to be inflamed with Christ's love.

The good St. Lucy on being scornfully asked by the governor of her city, "Is this the Holy Ghost in you?" calmly replied: "They whose hearts are pure are the temples of the Holy Ghost." "But," persisted the wicked man, "I will cause you to fall into sin, and the Holy Ghost will leave you." To which the virgin responded: "And I, remaining faithful to God, will not consent to sin, that thus the Holy Spirit may redouble my reward."

Then the tyrant had her dragged to a place of infamy. But as no power on earth could move the pure virgin to commit sin, she was brought back again to her wicked tormentor, to whom she said: "You see now that I am the temple of the Holy Ghost, and that He protects me. Nothing evil can happen to me unless He permits it."

Children, let us, like St. Lucy, too, flee from sin. Only thus shall we become temples of the Holy Spirit and make ourselves fit for everlasting companionship with God, in the kingdom that has **no end.**

FIRST SUNDAY AFTER PENTECOST

Works of Mercy

Of all the fruits of the Holy Ghost, my dear children, none has been more esteemed by the saints of God than the precious one of Charity. That means we should be kind-hearted, merciful, loving. "If you have charity for others," says St. Augustine, "you will wish only what is good for them." While another writer adds: "Humility does not see the faults of others, and charity does not disclose them."

Let it be a principle of your lives, my children, not to judge the actions of your neighbor as wrong, even though they appear sinful. Think to yourselves: "Perhaps if I were placed in those circumstances I might be just as bad, if not worse." If you reason thus, you will be meriting a merciful judgment for yourselves, for Christ has said distinctly: "With what measure you mete, it shall be measured against you again."

A certain monk, lying on his deathbed, appeared so cheerful and joyous that the abbot of the monastery in which he resided wondered exceedingly. "How is this?" he asked the dying man. "In all probability you will soon be summoned before the judgment seat of God, and yet you are so light-hearted!" "Father," replied the monk, "whenever my brethren have annoyed me or wronged me in any way, I have made it a practice to put the best possible construction on their words and actions. Now, since I have never judged others uncharitably, I venture to hope that I may find mercy in the presence of my Divine Judge."

Always remember, my dear children, that he who does not forgive his neighbor need not expect pardon from almighty God. This is our daily petition in the Our Father: "Forgive us our trespasses as we forgive those who trespass against us." Do we not pray, then, if we are unrelenting towards our neighbors, that God may be unrelenting towards us?

In the course of one of his sermons the late Archbishop Ryan once related this incident: "During the Civil War two Sisters of Charity while walking one day through the streets of Boston were insulted by a man who was intolerant of everything religious. It happened that, as time passed, this man entered the army, was wounded in one of the Missouri battles, and was brought to a temporary hospital in charge of these good sisters, where he was most kindly treated.

"When he was about to die, the sister who attended him begged him to make his peace with God. 'Sister,' replied the dying soldier, 'it is true I have been a bad man, but there is one act of my life weighing more heavily on my conscience than any other. Once I insulted a member of your holy Order. Were she only here now I would fall at her feet, ask her forgiveness, and die in peace.'

" 'Be comforted,' replied the sister, 'she has already pardoned you. The moment you were brought in here I recognized you by the mark on your forehead, but long ago I pardoned you from my heart.'

" 'And why,' rejoined the soldier, 'have you been, if anything, kinder to me than the others?'

" 'Because you insulted me so much for His sake,' she responded, kissing her crucifix.

" 'Then send at once for your priest,' begged the dying man. 'The religion that inspires such acts must surely come from God.'

"And the priest and the sister knelt together as the soul of the poor soldier passed before his Maker."

When you see anyone in need of your assistance, my children, either for body or soul, do not ask yourself why someone else did not offer the desired aid, but thank God that He has given you a chance of exercising charity.

It was a custom of St. Peter Claver to leave his home about Easter time to search the mountains for the negroes that might be scattered in their recesses. Though the tropical storms drenched him to the skin, he never faltered—never turned back. When he discovered a settlement he would remain there till the last negro had made his Easter duty.

Once it was noticed that he suddenly left home and plunged without a guide into the mountain fastnesses. No one knew where he went, but when he returned, pale and worn, it was learned that he had gone to administer the last Sacraments to three old negroes who, having been abandoned by all the world, had crawled into a delapidated hut to die.

Charity such as St. Peter Claver's, my children, is what we call heroic charity; it means to love one's neighbor more than one's self. Sometimes, thank God, we have instances of it even at the present day when the world seems to have grown, unfortunately, more selfish than formerly.

Some years ago—in January, 1889, to be more exact—a ship was wrecked off the Philippine Islands. Amid all the confusion after the vessel struck the rock, two Catholic missionaries were seen calmly assisting the passengers to board the life-boats. Then a quick warning was given them to leave the sinking ship. The call came not a moment too soon. One missionary obeyed the injunction—

the other was left on the fated vessel. As the waves closed over the massive framework the priest was seen praying to God, on its deck.

Some of the crew managed to keep afloat by swimming. One man, however, finding his strength failing him, swam up to the little craft in which the surviving missionary sat, and begged to be taken in. Already the boat was crowded, but the good priest, saying, "He can have my place," sprang into the water and disappeared beneath the waves.

Was not that heroic charity? If only our world possessed more of this precious gift, it would be a far better place than it is.

To love our neighbor, my dear children, is only another means of growing in the love of God. But you must not think this supernatural charity is easy; far from it. It costs many a sacrifice, yet it is worth them all. It means life-effort, life-struggle—but the crown awaiting the victor will be more than sufficient recompense.

SECOND SUNDAY AFTER PENTECOST

A Royal Banquet

My Dear Children: Our blessed Lord to-day takes us by the hand and tenderly leads us into a large supper-room. On the table are spread viands and delicious meats with which to refresh the weary body. But, strange to say, the room is not filled with guests. What means the empty table? Invitations have been sent far and wide, yet they have been unheeded. What care have the invited guests about the Lord's supper? Pride, avarice and sensuality are laying their snares to lure the human heart in other directions, and the weakling is only too eager to follow the call of the world. But what about ourselves? Let us look the matter squarely in the face. Are we, the favored little ones of the Lord's household, true to the Master's call, or do we, too, with so many others seek the broad road that leadeth to destruction? O, my children, let us not stay away from the Eucharistic banquet to which our Lord so lovingly invites us. This heavenly Food, so truly the life of our souls, will strengthen us in the combat and make us victorious over our enemies—the world, the flesh, and the devil.

An old soldier once had a collection of medals and pictures adorning the walls of his room, in which collection was one little print, soiled, torn, and so faded that one could hardly discover what it was. A friend coming to visit him one day, and scanning his souvenirs, asked: "What is this, so old and faded, that apparently holds the place of honor among all your treasures?"

"That," answered the aged man, "is the most precious of them all. The picture I received at my first Holy Communion—it is the sign of the promises I then made to God. It is faded because I carried it with me wherever I went. In the camp and on the battlefield, it never left me. When I was in trouble, I had only to raise my eyes to that talisman, and all sorrow vanished. New courage again became mine to face the battle of life. Now I am an old man. Soon I must die, but when that last hour comes, I hope that same picture, reminding me of my first Communion, will give me strength to meet the final struggle."

How tender must have been the relation, my dear children, between this good old soldier and his God! How lovingly must not that Divine Commander-in-chief have received this faithful army man at the last! Oh, let us imitate him and always retain the remembrance of our first Holy Communion! Let us not be among the number of those who refuse to come to the Eucharistic table—those who wish to be called followers of Christ—and yet whose hearts have room for naught else save the sinful pleasures of the world.

St. Francis of Sales, speaking of those who neglect to approach the Sacraments, says: "Those Christians who are lost will have nothing to answer to their Judge when He shall show them that they have been condemned to eternal punishment through their own fault."

On every one God bestows His favors, my children, yet all do not respond to His fatherly care. Not only the perfect are called to this royal banquet, but also those who are weak and deficient in virtue. There they may receive the God of strength, who will enable them to battle manfully with temptation and sin.

Not many years ago, during the Crimean War, a French officer, a man of great piety, happened to receive an order to attack one of the enemy's strongholds. Immediately he was seen at the head of his men, rushing forward to the assault. Though the onslaught was terrific, still, midst the glittering bayonets and showers of bullets, the officer could be seen, calm and apparently unconcerned, directing the movements of his ranks. By his bravery the fort was at length captured. His general, having viewed from a distance the entire attack, at the conclusion of the siege came to meet him with the words: "What bravery was yours, colonel! Where did you learn such calmness in the midst of danger so great?" "Why, general," he modestly replied, "there is but one answer to your question—I received Holy Communion this morning." Admiration for so much genuine piety and devotion filled the hearts of all who heard the courageous response.

Those who on account of worldly cares and sinful lives neglect to receive this heavenly Bread, my children, run the greatest risk of being deprived of the reception of this Sacrament in the hour of death. And justly; for it is but natural that Jesus should refuse to be in death the food of those ungrateful souls who have turned Him away in life, when He so lovingly looked for their companionship. Resolve, then, as long as you live, to go frequently to Holy Communion, that you may increase more and more your fear and love of God.

It is told of a certain artist, who in his youth had led a life of dissipation, but who had returned to the service of God, that in order to atone for his past sinful excesses, he made the resolution to receive Holy Communion every Sunday henceforth. Never did he willingly break his pious resolve. On one occasion, with great simplicity and confidence, he said to the bishop of his diocese: "For my part, I do not fear death. I receive Holy Communion with the best dispositions in my power, so that the grim slayer, when he knocks at my door, will not find me unprepared." As a final word, my dear children, let me exhort you to frequent the Holy Table, after having first cleansed your soul from all defilement in the saving Sacrament of Penance. Thus you will ever be ready to meet your God!

THIRD SUNDAY AFTER PENTECOST

The Erring Sheep

Most pleasing to the Heart of Jesus, my dear children, was this scathing taunt of the Pharisees: "This man receiveth sinners and eateth with them." Yes, our Messias, our Holy One, was proud to be the friend of sinners. He came not to condemn but to save—and so, as if in answer to their mocking words, He uttered the parable which we find recorded in to-day's Gospel: "What man is there of you that hath a hundred sheep, and if he shall lose one of them, doth he not leave the ninety-nine in the desert, and go after that which was lost, until he find it?" The sinner, then, our blessed Lord compares to a sheep. As the latter sometimes leaves the fold seeking the freedom of the fastnesses of the forest far away from the shepherd's care, so the sinner overpowered and delighted by the good things of earth often wanders from the path of duty and strays far from the protecting hand of his God.

A shepherd boy, once guarding his flock in a mountain region, being wearied by long vigils, fell asleep while sitting on a rock. A ram close by, seeing the boy continually nodding his head and thinking that he was thus challenging him to a fight, butted him with his horns. Thoroughly angered by being aroused from his sleep in so rude a fashion, the shepherd seized the ram by the horns and flung the animal over a jutting cliff. Hardly had the sheep, a hundred in number, noticed this, when, true to instinct, they followed the ram, and fell headlong over the precipice.

Here is a vivid example, my children, of the sinner following his guide, the world. Blindfolded as it were, he rushes on to ultimate destruction.

But the sheep have usually a faithful shepherd, who, ever anxious about his flock, watches carefully lest any should wander astray. If one is missing, immediately he goes in search of it. Just so does the Good Shepherd of our souls act. Far more watchful than any earthly shepherd, our loving Saviour persistently seeks the wayward sheep, and having found it, brings it back on His shoulders, rejoicing.

During the French Revolution there lived at Lyons a man who for many years had discarded religious practices of all kinds. It happened one day that he saw a priest carrying the Blessed Sacrament to a sick person. In order to avoid meeting him, the man straightway turned into another street, but great was his astonishment to find that the clergyman with his precious burden was going the same way. Again the man tried a different road, yet with like success. Ever the footsteps of the minister of God could be heard coming nearer and nearer. At last the wayward one took refuge in an open doorway, only to see the priest directing his steps towards him, for in that very house lived the sick person. At this moment, Divine grace flooding his soul, he exclaimed: "See how God's mercy is pursuing me! I shall not resist any longer. From this very hour I believe as firmly as of old." And his conversion was complete.

In the parable cited our blessed Lord closes with the beautiful words: "So I say to you, there shall be joy before the angels of God upon one sinner doing penance." Nothing then should keep us from making our peace with our Creator, if we have been so unfortunate as to have strayed from His keeping! Oh! let us return quickly to Him, my children, if ever we are so rash as to wander away!

A certain young man, having for a long time lived a life of dissipation and sin, filled the measure of his iniquities one evening by going out in an open field and, in his madness, pointing his drawn dagger to heaven, challenging God to a duel. "Come down and show your power!" he mockingly cried. "See whether you are able to destroy me!"

And behold what happened! A piece of white paper floating in the air fell right at the feet of the irreligious man. Picking it up, he saw "Miserere mei, Deus," printed in letters of gold.

Overwhelmed by the prodigy and the thought of God's mercy, the young man's heart was filled with the deepest sorrow and compunction. Ever afterwards he strove to lead a holy life, and he had the happiness of dying a happy death.

My dear children, the mercy of our good Lord haunts us at every step. An accident happens: God is calling us to look into ourselves, to examine our lives, and to realize that the root of all our misfortunes lies within us. We are afflicted with a fatal disease: God is seeking our bedside to cause us to turn our eyes toward the condition of our soul; perhaps its state is far worse than that of our infirm body. We retire at night, and while on our bended knees, God raises the veil, so to speak, and reminds us that this very night perhaps we may be in eternity. Ever is our Good Shepherd sounding the note of warning. Well for us if we hearken to His voice!

FOURTH SUNDAY AFTER PENTECOST

The Word of God and the Word of Parents

Surely, my dear children, there was never a greater orator on earth than the God-Man, Jesus of Nazareth! Notice how the Gospel expressly states: "The multitude pressed upon Jesus to hear the word of God." From far and near they came, eager to catch the tones of that gentle Voice that swayed the world—eager to receive a blessing from the uplifted Hand that ruled the universe. For days sometimes they followed where He led. Hunger, thirst, weariness, mattered nothing, just so they might be in the presence of the Master!

How these good people put us of the present generation to shame! Nothing will debar them from hearing the word of God, while we are only too anxious to escape the strain of a sermon. Yes, "strain," that is the word we sometimes use when in reality we ought to fall down on our knees and thank God we are living in a land where it is our privilege to listen to sermons! Not yet has the hand of persecution been lifted against us here in America. But the day may come, and we know not how soon, when caves and caverns may be our resort to hear the word of God. And then we will be longing for it and cannot have it! Poor blinded mortals we are indeed, if we will not give a meagre half hour on Sunday to listen with dutiful heart to God's sublime teaching!

It happened one day that as St. Louis Bertrand and another holy man were strolling along a country road, conversing on pious subjects, a youth was hurriedly walking a short distance behind them. Under his cloak he carried a sword, while the resolve to kill seemed to be imprinted on his very features. Without taking any notice of the approach of the young man, St. Louis continued to speak in a loud tone as before. Suddenly, to the great surprise of both religious, the youth, throwing away his concealed weapon, cast himself at the feet of the saint, with the words: "Ah, my Father, may God reward you for what you have done for me to-day!" To the holy man's expression of astonishment the youth replied: "I was on my way to take revenge on my bitter enemy. But the words I heard from your lips have so changed my heart that I am now on my knees to ask pardon of God."

"My son, do you forgive from your heart him who has injured you?" asked St. Louis.

"Yes, Father, from my inmost soul," was the quick response.

"Then God will also forgive you," answered the holy man.

Thus reconciled to his Saviour, the youth from that day persevered in the new life of grace, so wonderfully conferred on him for having listened attentively to God's holy word.

There is, however, another lesson taught in to-day's Gospel, my dear children—the lesson of prompt obedience. When our Lord's discourse to those humble people of Judea was finished, He commanded Simon Peter: "Launch out into the deep, and let down your nets for a draught." St. Peter's reply is characteristic of the man deemed worthy by our Lord to be the first holy Pontiff: "Master, we have labored all the night, and have taken nothing, but at Thy word I will let down the net." Think of that, my children: Peter had labored all the night with no success, yet he does not for a moment question the Lord's command. Here is a beautiful example for you. Do you always follow the instructions and commands of your parents and superiors as promptly as this frank fisherman obeyed the simple wish of his Master, Jesus? I am afraid not. Nowadays it is the common complaint of parents that their children obey them only when they feel like it. Have you never read that in the Old Testament those guilty of disobedience were taken outside the city walls and stoned? And our dear Lord will also punish you for disregarding the instructions of those to whose care you have been confided.

Not very long ago a certain boy was sent by his parents to a leading school of Paris to be educated. Before leaving home his good mother gave him this parting word of advice: "My child, I will no longer be able to watch over you as I have done heretofore. Promise me that you will always study your catechism and say your prayers devoutly. Keep away from bad companions, and neglect none of your religious duties." Obediently the boy gave his mother the assurance that he would do all she directed him.

Entering the college, he innocently formed the acquaintance of two boys of his own age, who soon ensnared their new friend and taught him all manner of wickedness. It was not long till prayers and catechism were things of the past. He actually became worse than his companions. On one occasion, having committed a very serious fault, he was as a punishment confined to his room for several hours. When the time had expired the principal went to free him from his isolation, but on approaching the door he was surprised at the oppressive silence reigning there. On entering, imagine his terror and sorrow to find the lifeless body of the boy hanging from a beam in the roof!

Such, my dear children, was the terrible ending of one who failed to follow the injunction of his good mother!

"Cursed be he who honoreth not his father and mother," are the words of Holy Scripture. And these are not unmeaning words, my dear boys and girls, only a short time ago this Divine curse fell most disastrously upon the son and daughter of a noble family who by every means in their power had embittered their parents' lives. The son was maimed by a horse, so that he became a cripple for life; the daughter was afflicted with a serious illness which left her totally blind.

From these examples, my children, you should learn how severely God punishes disobedience. If, however, you follow your parents' injunctions joyfully and willingly—remembering that they take God's place in your regard—then many blessings here on earth, and eternal beatitude hereafter, will assuredly be yours!

FIFTH SUNDAY AFTER PENTECOST

Hypocrisy. Charity Towards Our Neighbor

"Except your justice abound more than that of the scribes and Pharisees, you shall not enter into the kingdom of heaven." In such words, my dear children, does our blessed Lord show that the justice of the scribes and Pharisees was not acceptable to Him. On more than one occasion He openly rebuked these teachers of the people for not practising themselves what they required of others. He Who was gentleness and tenderness personified, even goes so far as to call these wretched men the wearers of the conspicuous mark, "Hypocrites." Hypocrisy, then, my children, is a vice our Redeemer seems to detest more than all others—that pretense that we are better than we really are. How do we ourselves regard a man who pretends to be better than he is? Do we not despise him? Do we not feel an unmistakable aversion to his company? And how can this abominable trait take such utter possession of the human heart? If only we were masters of the lesson so beautifully taught by the author of the Imitation, how near perfection we would be!

St. James, Bishop of Nisibis, was one day traveling through the country when he was accosted by a beggar manifesting great piety. The latter, approaching the Saint, tearfully implored him to bestow on him an alms for the purpose of burying his companion, who, he said, had just expired by the roadside. With entire confidence in his sincerity, the holy Bishop gave him what he asked, and then proceeded on his way, praying earnestly for the soul of the deceased. The beggar rejoicing in the thought of having imposed on the Saint so easily, ran back to his companion whom he had left at some distance, lying on the ground as if dead. Drawing near the spot, he called his comrade to come and enjoy with him his readily-won alms, but to his consternation he received no answer. Approaching nearer, he found his partner really dead. Immediately he again sought the Saint, and casting himself on his knees, he acknowledged his deceit and implored pardon. The servant of God, having first reproved him for his sin, betook himself to prayer. At his intercession, the unhappy man who had provoked the Almighty to inflict such a punishment upon him, was restored to life and became a sincere penitent.

In another part of the Gospel read in the Mass to-day we find the words: "Whosoever is angry with his brother shall be in danger of the judgment." Again, therefore, as on many previous occasions, does our Lord recommend charity to our neighbor. Never say an injurious word of another, nor make fun at a companion's humiliation. And above all, never ridicule the aged on account of infirmity or poverty. Remember, my children, a day may come when you too will be old, when you will bless the one who offers you a helping hand. Think of that day now, and "Do unto others as you would have them do unto you." Do you not recollect, from your Bible History the punishment meted out by an angry God when bad boys called the prophet Eliseus disrespectful names? What happened? History tells us that two large bears issued from the woods and devoured the wicked children. Be this then your life's principle—protect and help your neighbor whenever you can; have pity on the unfortunate, on those worsted in the battle of life. Only in this way can you assure yourself to be the friend of God.

St. Peter Paschal, having been captured by Mahometans, was thrown into prison. His friends, on hearing of his plight and the cruel treatment he was receiving, sent a large sum of money for his ransom. But instead of spending it for his own deliverance, he immediately freed by its means a number of women and children who were in danger of losing their faith.

Pleased with this heroic act of charity, our Lord one morning at Mass came in person to thank him. A little boy, clothed in the garment of a slave, having served his Mass, the Saint as was his wont, before he dismissed the child asked him some questions of the catechism. So accurate were the answers he received that the holy man marvelled at the knowledge of one so young. Finally, when he said, "Who is Jesus Christ?" the child unhesitatingly answered: "I am Jesus Christ. Look at My hands, feet and side, and you will see the marks of the nails and spear. As you in your charity have become a server for the sake of My people, so I have made Myself your server." Saying these words, the Divine Child disappeared, leaving the Saint in an ecstasy of joy.

Again our blessed Lord exhorts us: "If, therefore, thou offer thy gift at the altar, and there thou remember that thy brother hath anything against thee, leave there thy offering before the altar, and go first to be reconciled to thy brother; and then coming, thou shalt offer thy gift." Thus our Saviour teaches us always to pardon for His sake those who have offended us.

A little boy, a companion of the blessed Sebastian, once having had a quarrel with another child, entertained for some time his feeling of anger. When Sebastian heard of this, he resolved to be the means of bringing about a reconciliation between his little comrades. Going to his friend, he inquired if he had said the "Our Father" that morning. The boy, not knowing the reason of Sebastian's question, replied: "Why, yes; of course I did." To which Sebastian responded: "Then surely you did not notice the words,

'Forgive us our trespasses as we forgive those who trespass against us!'" Realizing his fault, the boy at once begged pardon of God and sought the child with whom he had quarrelled to solicit forgiveness.

Two lessons then, my children, we are to learn from to-day's Gospel: The first is that we should appear before men as we are before God—no feigning, no hypocrisy. The second, that we must habituate ourselves to the virtue of charity, remembering the words of our Divine Lord: "By this shall all men know that you are My disciples, if you have love one for another."

SIXTH SUNDAY AFTER PENTECOST

The Holy Sacrifice of the Mass

What excessive love, my dear children, does not our blessed Saviour exhibit towards us, His sinful creatures! Knowing that as long as we live in this world, we are in the midst of a desert where there is nothing that will satisfy our souls, He has amply provided for us by giving us His doctrine, His grace, and His Sacraments. All this He does by the ministry of His priests.

But the most sublime act of these, His ministers, is the Holy Sacrifice of the Mass. There our good Lord multiplies for us that heavenly Food which He has left to be the nourishment of our souls. As once in the wilderness when the people had been with Him for three days and had nothing to eat, He said to His disciples: "I have compassion on the multitude. . . . If I shall send them away fasting to their homes, they will faint on the way," so now He has compassion on us also and recognizes the need of each individual soul gathered before Him. And to supply that need He instituted the Holy Sacrifice of the Mass. From the beginning of the world, even as far back as the time of Cain and Abel, we find that sacrificial offerings were made, either as an act of homage to the Lord of the world, or else as an act of reparation to appease an angry God. In the Old Law the sacrifices were bloody; in the New, Jesus Christ offers Himself in an unbloody manner by the hands of the priest, as atonement for the living and the dead.

Towards the middle of the thirteenth century a certain priest, by name Jone Perez, along with many others, was taken captive by the Moors. "Who are you?" queried the barbarian ruler, when the priest was brought into his presence, for he noticed that the dress of this man differed much from that of the people, and his face betokened superior rank.

"I am a Christian, and a Catholic priest," was the reply. "What is a Catholic priest?" asked the Emir. "The priest of the true God," answered Father Perez, "ordained for a sublime ministry. His power surpasses that of the greatest king, for by uttering certain words He is able to change bread into the body of the King of Heaven and earth, and wine into His Blood."

The Emir and his courtiers smiled, yet, wanting to test the priest, the Emir commanded him to perform this mysterious rite. The minister of God, though anxious to yield to the request, said that as he had none of the necessaries for the Holy Mass, the Emir would be obliged to send a messenger to Cuenta, a town some distance away, if he wished his command to be obeyed. Immediately the messenger was despatched, returning a few days afterwards with all that was necessary for the Holy Sacrifice.

On the following morning, the feast of the Exaltation of the Holy Cross, the priest prepared to celebrate Mass, but as there was no figure of Christ on the Cross presented to him, he hesitated to begin. God, however, in His wonderful Providence, came to his assistance. Two angels entering by a window in the tower approached the altar in the presence of the Emir and his nobles, and placed in the hands of the celebrant a crucifix, at the same time informing the priest that within the case was a relic of the true Cross.

Filled with awe and astonishment at what he had seen, the Emir kept his eyes riveted on the priest at the altar. His amazement increased all the more when, after the words of consecration, he beheld in the Sacred Host, Jesus, under the form of a beautiful child. The Holy Sacrifice being completed, he asked the priest to instruct him in the doctrines of the Catholic religion and not long afterwards he himself and his entire people were baptized. He died at the age of forty-two, on the feast of the Exaltation of the Holy Cross, having persevered to the end in his pious sentiments.

Since this Holy Sacrifice, my children, is the greatest act of our faith, and our chief means of obtaining all graces and blessings, we need not wonder at the anxiety of the Saints to assist at it. When St. Felix was but twelve years old, he was even then accustomed to go very frequently to the Sacraments, and to hear Mass daily. In order that he might receive the manifold blessings granted to those who assist at the Holy Sacrifice, he used to consign his flock of sheep (for he was only a shepherd boy) to the care of his heavenly Father. Nor did our good God fail him; pleased with this filial confidence, he oftentimes sent an angel from heaven to guard the lambs committed to His Divine protection. Even the people of the country asserted that while Felix was absent, they saw a shepherd guarding his flock—a boy of the child's own age, but unknown to everybody. In the course of time this miracle was discovered, and people began to feel a holy reverence for the little shepherd boy.

Let me conclude, my children, with urging you never to miss Mass through your own fault. Sickness should be your only excuse. If in this matter you imitate the example of the saints, you like them shall reap the same reward: the heavenly blessings promised to those who assist devoutly at this, the sublimest act of our holy faith.

SEVENTH SUNDAY AFTER PENTECOST

Scandal

"Beware of false prophets who come to you in the clothing of sheep, but inwardly they are ravening wolves."

Would you believe, my children, that even in the fold of Christ, in His Church, there are people well instructed in His doctrine, who all their lives have experienced naught but mercy and kindness from Him, and yet who disseminate error and heresy among their associates? Such people are Christians only in name. It is in order to merit the praises of men that they perform their good works; they do nothing for the glory of God. These false teachers claim that sin is nothing more than forbidden pleasure; that such unlawful restrictions ought not to be placed on human kind; that everyone has a right to enjoy the world as much as in him lies. But, my children, beware; they are indeed "false prophets," bad Christians, who teach such error!

Saint Augustine, before his conversion, led a life of unrestrained dissipation, reviling the things of God and seeking only the pleasures of the world. In his "Confessions" we find the following striking illustration of his influence: "When I was at Tagastus," he writes, "I met there a young man for whom I conceived an ardent affection. Both of the same age, our dispositions were such that we seemed to have been born for one another. So deep was his love for me that I soon saw he would do anything whatever I asked of him; and realizing my influence, I proposed to him to renounce the Catholic faith. He did it without demur for my sake."

St. Augustine goes on to relate that after they had lived thus about a year, entirely content in each other's company, the young man suddenly became ill and was brought to the point of death. Day and night Augustine sat at his bedside waiting for a sign of recognition from his unconscious friend. At last, when he had so far recovered as to know those attending him, his eyes fell on Augustine. "As soon as he recognized me," writes the holy Bishop, "he sadly turned away his eyes and declared that if I still desired to be his friend I must henceforth abstain from reviling the Catholic faith. Though at first I was annoyed at his request, the grace of God soon gained the mastery over my depraved heart, and realizing the evil I had done in drawing a soul away from its Creator, I left his bedside to weep over my sins."

It is a very easy matter, my dear children, to give scandal; a bad word, an act or a gesture may suffice to encourage others to fall. Do not think lightly, then, of your exterior conduct. Watch over your every action lest you should be the means of leading anyone astray.

There was once a young lady who, though always very pious and good, yet had her defects. Inclined to be vain, she took pleasure in hearing herself admired. It came to pass that, being taken seriously ill, she was warned that her death was very near, but like a good Christian she received this news with calm resignation. To her companions surrounding her bedside she spoke these few parting words of advice: "My friends, to you who have been my constant associates, I say now, though kindly, that your company has done me no good. I wish we had all been different. Only a little while longer, and I must leave this world, to give an account of all those vain actions and conversations in which I frittered away my time. Take my advice: Shun the company of those who are vain, proud and worldly; by such means can Satan drag you into sin. My last request is that you pray for me that God may forgive my transgressions, especially the vain, foolish and worldly actions by which I have offended Him."

If you have ever committed the grave sin of scandal, my dear children, you must make reparation for it, and thereby appease God for the wrong committed. Our heavenly Father often punishes this sin by giving the transgressor no time for atonement.

My children, always remember the words of our blessed Lord about those who give scandal: "It were better that a millstone be hanged about the neck of such a one, and that he be drowned in the depths of the sea. For it must needs be that scandals come, but woe to the one by whom the scandal cometh." When such a condemnation has been pronounced by the lips of Jesus Christ Himself, it is a clear proof that he who scandalizes one of His trusting little ones is deserving of eternal damnation.

EIGHTH SUNDAY AFTER PENTECOST

The Fruit of Almsgiving

My dear Children: Look around the world to-day and you will surely notice two great divisions in our social organizations—two classes of people living in widely different spheres of life: the rich and the poor. There are those who possess millions, who glory in their real estate, pleasure yachts, automobiles and palatial residences—and there are those who have none of these thing, who live from hand to mouth, content if they have only sufficient to keep the breath of life in their emaciated bodies—God's poor! Our Lord Himself has said: "The poor you have always with you."

No matter how rich we are, my children, we should remember that our wealth does not truly belong to us: it is the property of almighty God. We are only the managers of that which we hold. Therefore it should be our constant endeavor to give largely of this world's goods to those who are in a lower sphere of life, financially, than we are. Does not Christ say to those who neglect to give alms to His poor: "Depart from Me, ye cursed, into everlasting fire, for I was hungry and you gave Me not to eat; naked, and you covered Me not"? And our Lord wants us to distinctly understand that when we are generous to the poor it is to Himself we are bounteous. Here are His very words: "As long as you did it to one of these My least brethren, you did it to Me." Learn, therefore, my children, to help God's poor, to love those in distress and to offer them your assistance, even if it be not much. How admirable it is to see a child possess this generous spirit, willing to give of its smallest treasure to help the needy.

Saint Antonius never refused an alms asked in the name of God. When he had no money he freely distributed his garments and household furniture among the poor. One day, being sent by the Florentines on an embassy to the sovereign Pontiff, he met near the gates of Rome a beggar who asked for an alms for Christ's sake. Outdoing St. Martin in generosity, St. Antonius gave the man his whole cloak. When he entered the city another was given him; by whom he knew not.

The rewards of almsgiving are often most remarkable, my children, for God will not be surpassed in generosity. Not only extraordinary temporal favors are conferred upon the bounteous giver, but also manifold spiritual blessings.

Alfred, King of England, having lost his kingdom, at one time had to take refuge in a poor hut, where, despite their privations, he lived happily with his queen. One day a beggar knocked at this door and asked for something to eat. "What have we left?" inquired Alfred of his wife. "But one loaf of bread," she replied. "Thanks be to God," said the king. "He Who fed five thousand people with a few loaves, will also feed us with half a one; give the other half to the beggar." His generosity was soon rewarded, for a little while afterwards a peasant brought a large dish of fish to the king's hut.

In the following year Alfred took up arms against his enemies and recovered his kingdom. The signal victories he gained seemed to be temporal favors bestowed on him for his admirable life of self-abnegation, while his adversaries were in power.

Sometimes almsgiving, though bestowed with a half-reluctant spirit, disposes the heart to true contrition and a firm purpose of amendment. This is well illustrated by the following little story: Almost starved, a poor beggar one day asked a miser for a piece of bread. For a long time the latter paid no attention to the mendicant, but finally, to rid himself of his importunity, he threw him a small loaf. The following night the miser had a strange dream: He seemed to be standing before his God, his Judge, while the devil counted up his misdeeds. In vain did his good angel seek for something meritorious to insure his salvation. At last, finding the loaf of bread given in charity to the poor man, the angel put it on the scale, and lo! it outweighed all his transgressions! It was only a dream, but nevertheless it had its good effect: the miser thereafter became a generous, kind-hearted man.

All during his holy life John the Almoner was renowned for his bountiful charity to the poor. To convince himself of the saint's generosity, a rich man once clothed himself in tattered garments and stationed himself in front of the hospital which the Almoner was accustomed to pass. As soon as he noticed the holy man he cried out: "Have mercy on me, for I am wretched, having just been freed from prison." Turning to his servant who carried his money, St. John said: "Give this man six pieces of silver." The stranger having received the offering, thanked his benefactor and went away. As soon as the saint was out of sight, the rich man again changed his unseemly clothes, donned others, and meeting the servant of God on another street, said: "Take pity on me, Father, for I am in great need." This time seven pieces of money were given him. Under a different guise, for a third time the man presented himself for an alms, whereupon the saint's servant thus addressed him: "This is the third time to-day, Father, that this beggar has importuned you. What shall I do?" "Give him twelve pieces of silver," was the reply, "for it may be Jesus Christ Himself Who has assumed the guise to try Me." Thus was the rich man convinced of John the Almoner's patience and charity. Returning home, he felt full of veneration for one of such eminent sanctity.

Therefore be kind and charitable to the poor, my children. It always pays. "Make friends of the Mammon of iniquity" for the good of others. Thus will you merit for yourselves the loving word of our blessed Saviour: "Come, ye blessed of My Father, possess ye the kingdom, which was prepared for you from the foundation of the world."

NINTH SUNDAY AFTER PENTECOST

THE OBSTINATE SINNER. THE HOUSE OF GOD

"If thou also hadst known, and that in this thy day, the things that are to thy peace, but now they are hidden from thy eyes."

So spoke our blessed Lord on that eventful day when He drew near ungrateful Jerusalem, and wept over it; and so also, my dear children, does He admonish in tender words the obstinate sinner who continues to revel in his wickedness. The wrongdoer fain would enjoy peace of heart, but the gratification of his passions prevents him, and the thought of the just punishment to be meted out to his evil deeds eventually drives him to despair.

In the days of St. Francis Borgia there lived in Spain a man addicted to every sinful crime. Suddenly a severe sickness came upon him. Those of his friends who had still remained faithful to God, seeing that his malady was a dangerous one, urged him to be reconciled to his Maker, but to no avail. He laughingly assured them: "There is plenty of time."

St. Francis being told of the man's condition and realizing the danger in which he stood of losing his soul, kneeling down before a crucifix, begged our loving Saviour not to allow that soul to perish. In answer to his prayer a voice from the crucifix said: "Go, Francis, and exhort the dying man to repent." Immediately the saint went, but though he reasoned with the obstinate sinner for a long time, nothing could induce the latter to confess his sins. Again Francis betook himself to prayer, and again he returned to the sick man's bedside, saying: "I come once more to urge you in the name of Jesus of Nazareth, Who died for you, to make your peace with God." As there was still no surrender to grace, the saint placed a crucifix before the eyes of the dying man. At that moment, by a miracle of God's mercy, the figure on the cross seemed to be covered with wounds from which the blood issued in copious streams. "Ah! my son," said St. Francis, "see how Jesus loves you, although you have so grievously offended Him," but the man, still refusing to accept the proffered grace, died impenitent as he had lived.

Thus you see, my dear children, that you will most certainly endanger your salvation if you reject the merciful hand outstretched to help you. Be very careful, therefore, in this matter, and never neglect to open the door of your heart when you hear God knocking for admission. If we thus profit by the call of our Lord during our sojourn here on earth, we shall not merit that reproach that He so justly addressed to ungrateful Jerusalem.

"And entering into the temple, He began to cast out them that sold therein, and them that bought, saying to them: 'It is written, My house is the house of prayer, but you have made it a den of thieves.'" I am very much afraid, my dear children, that God would have to act in a similar manner nowadays if He entered many of our churches. How often do we not see there young men and women laughing and talking instead of praying! In God's house where the body of our Lord is daily consecrated, where angels night and day adore the Prisoner of the Tabernacle, we should behave with a holy reverence. Faith tells us "Jesus is here," but how little, apparently, do we realize the stupendous mystery! If we but thought seriously of our belief, there would be no need to urge devotion in prayer.

In the state of Virginia, long ago, a ten-year-old boy who had misbehaved and caused a disturbance in church, was imprisoned and sentenced to a whipping, to be inflicted by his mother. Rather a severe punishment, you little boys and girls will say, for a slight offence. Slight? Is it slight, my children, when the God of heaven and earth is the insulted one?

Philip the Second, King of Spain, was one day in church with all his royal court. To his great displeasure he noticed during the Holy Sacrifice of the Mass two of his courtiers laughing and talking. Having summoned them into his presence after the services, he addressed them in these severe words: "Keep hereafter out of my sight! Have you not incurred the displeasure of the almighty King of heaven by your acts of irreverence in His holy House?" And forthwith they were dismissed from his court.

How much our duty is it not then, my dear children, to respect the place where the Lord dwells. Enter the church, therefore, with fear and trembling; it is the abode of the All-holy God! In the Old Testament Moses was commanded to strip the shoes off his feet when he approached to converse with his Creator, for, saith the Lord, "The spot whereon thou standest is holy ground." How much more to be revered, then, is the Catholic Church of to-day, containing in all its entirety the sanctuary of the Most High!

TENTH SUNDAY AFTER PENTECOST

Pride

"The Pharisee standing, prayed thus within himself: 'O God, I give Thee thanks that I am not as the rest of men. . . . I fast twice in the week; I give tithes of all that I possess.'"

What is the leading characteristic of this seemingly devout Pharisee, my children, as he stands thus in the temple communing with his God? A characteristic that destroys the good works of many Christians, nowadays—a trait of character that we must needs shun if we would be acceptable in the sight of our Maker—Pride. It is necessary for us all, young and old alike, to close our eyes to our own merits and occupy ourselves rather with the consideration of our constant sinfulness. Thus only will we avoid the despicable sin of pride, that vice which causes us to boast that "we are not like the rest of men": *we* have no faults, no vices.

The old fable about the ox and the frog very well exemplifies the foolishness of the proud: An ox was once grazing near a pond where a number of frogs had made their home. One of the latter seeing the large animal, spoke thus boastingly to his companions: "I can make myself as big as that ox." So he puffed himself up with all his might. This brought on him only the ridicule of the other frogs, since he was scarcely any bigger than before, despite all his trying. "You laugh at me," the foolish frog replied, "but I can make myself ever so much bigger," whereupon he puffed himself up until he burst.

Like this frog are those foolish persons who in the pride of their hearts magnify themselves and wish to be considered greater than they really are, and like him, they will only bring upon themselves shame and confusion instead of the glory they covet.

Pride was the cause of the fall of Lucifer and his rebel band from their thrones in heaven. Despite his angelic intelligence Lucifer thought that he was like to God, and for that sin of thought he was hurled into the dark abyss. Pride it was likewise that made our first parents long for the knowledge of good and evil, and what was the result? Banished from the Garden of Eden, they were condemned to eat their bread in the sweat of their brow. Not only that, but, by the fall of Adam and Eve, sin and death became the inheritance of the human race. And so, to-day, souls are still meriting eternal destruction by the sin of pride. Be careful, therefore, my children, to curb every arrogant thought, for pride is the root of all evil.

In the year 42 A. D., Herod Agrippa journeyed from Jerusalem to Caesarea to attend a solemn festival in honor of the Emperor Claudius, at which a large multitude from every part of the province was to be assembled. As was the custom in those times, games were held to do honor to the occasion. On the second day of the celebration, Herod, wearing a mantle of cloth of gold which shone with great brilliancy, betook himself to the amphitheatre to the magnificent throne prepared for him. When the people saw him thus attired, and heard him speak, they cried out in joyous acclamation: "It is the voice of a god, not a man, that we hear. Long live the god Herod!" And, running to the foot of his throne, they knelt down to adore him. Pleased with their base adulation, Herod accepted as his due the homage they offered him.

But the punishment of God soon overtook him. While he was still in the act of receiving their servile flattery, he was afflicted with a terrible illness, the pains of which were so unbearable that he cried out in his agony: "See! Your god is about to die!"

His attendants tenderly carried him to an adjoining apartment, while the splendid games were speedily brought to an end. Every moment his intense torments seemed to increase, till after five days of unintermitting suffering, the like of which has never been known in history, the unfortunate Herod died. His body was found to be one mass of corruption. Such was the tragic end of the proud man who had dared to mock Jesus Christ in His passion, and had deemed himself equal to God.

Pride not only vitiates the heart and renders it utterly incapable of feeling the sufferings and afflictions of sorrowing humanity, but it also destroys the merits of all other good works.

It is related that a pious father had accustomed himself to read the Holy Scriptures before retiring to rest, while his three sons said their night prayers. On one occasion two of the boys being unable to keep awake, the third thus addressed his father: "Look, father, my two brothers have fallen asleep whilst I have been saying my prayers." The man noticing the arrogant tone in his child's remark, promptly replied: "My boy, it were better for you to fall asleep at your prayers, than to boast of keeping awake!"

Therefore, my dear children, the good works on which we pride ourselves are worthless in God's sight. Let us then, instead of glorifying in our actions, rather strike our breasts and say, "O God, be merciful to me, a sinner!" Thus shall we too return to our homes justified, for "Every one that exalteth himself shall be humbled, and he that humbleth himself shall be exalted."

ELEVENTH SUNDAY AFTER PENTECOST

Impenitence

My Dear Children: To-day our Divine Lord is presented to us as performing another stupendous miracle, the cure of a deaf and dumb man, and we think within ourselves if only *we* had been the favored ones to live in that blessed time, how happy we would be to lay all the wounds of our souls beneath His gentle touch, that He might in His bountiful mercy cure them. Such pious longings, however, do not help us much on the road to perfection. It were better for us to study our spiritual infirmities and employ for their healing the means our ever-thoughtful Saviour has left in His Church.

The deaf mute whom these good people brought to our Lord that He might lay His hand upon him, is a figure of the inveterate sinner. Falling repeatedly into sin, his relapses become second nature to him, while he grows deaf to the voice of God and speechless to His representative who might so easily cure him of his infirmities.

Saint Martin tells us of some blind men who in his own time were accustomed to stand near a certain church to beg. When, however, they heard that the holy man was coming that way, they immediately dispersed, fearful that he might cure them, for he was renowned for his miracles.

Many young people, my children, resemble these blind men. They do not want to be healed of their spiritual afflictions. They are afraid of coming in contact with some good soul who might convert them; therefore they avoid church, prayer, or any good act that might lead them to God. They love sin for its own sake, and for the pleasure they derive from committing it. How terrible it is to be in this state!

One day a holy monk was favored by a vision of his angel guardian walking at his side. As they went along, they passed a carcass of a dead animal lying by the wayside, from which the stench was so noisome that the very air was infected. The monk unable to endure the bad odor, hurried on his way as fast as he could, but the angel did not seem to notice the odor.

When they had gone some distance, they met a young man coming toward them, arrayed in the most costly garments. As soon as the angel saw him, his countenance grew very sad, and hastening his steps, he quickly passed him, in the meantime keeping his eyes fixed away from the man. The monk, inquiring of the angel why he exhibited such disgust on meeting this youth when he had showed no signs of displeasure on passing the carcass, received this reply: "The sight and smell of the dead animal were indeed bad; yet if you saw, as we angels see, the terrible state of that young man's soul, you would die from fright."

Oh! my children, keep away from sin, since it makes your soul so hideous in the sight of God, and causes you to resist all Divine influence.

A Christian is spiritually deaf and dumb when he remains inexorable in his sinful ways, and is unyielding in spite of warnings, threats or punishments. Such persons harden their hearts against the voice of God and sink into a state of obduracy that is one of the most frightful chastisements of the Almighty.

Long before the Last Supper, Judas had been sinning by avarice and deceit. In his heart he had already outlined his plan for the betrayal of his Saviour. Gentle chiding, tender reproaches, had no effect, but still the merciful Jesus condoned. When, finally, "Satan entered into him," as Holy Scripture relates, Judas went and hanged himself.

The example of Judas, my children, ought to teach us that the hardened sinner often dies impenitent. Wishing to know nothing of confession and conversion, he passes before the judgment seat of God with his many sins upon him.

St. Gregory the Great relates that there was once a wealthy man who lived only for the world and its pleasures, never caring for the interests of his immortal soul. What was worse, he had a large family whom he had trained in his own evil practices. At length, having become ill, his body was racked with excruciating pain, but the sufferings of his soul were infinitely greater. Before his eyes hovered his long list of sins. Already he seemed to see the evil spirits congregated around his bed. Wherever he looked the same terrible spectres appeared, so that he cried out in his agony. Finally, calling his oldest son, Maximus, to his bedside, he said in heartrending tones: "My dear son, oh! think of all I have done for you, and help me now! Save me from these terrible demons surrounding me!" But Maximus did not understand. In haste he called together his relatives, telling them his father's mind was wandering. "No," exclaimed the dying man, "my mind is not wandering. See, they are overwhelming me!" And he tried to raise himself from his bed, but was too weak to move. With the words: "Oh, give me another day!" he died in an agony of despair.

Learn this lesson, my children, to guard against spiritual deafness and dumbness. Be always ready to confess all your sins without exception honestly and truthfully, and listen attentively to the advice of your spiritual director. Thus will you avoid that deplorable condition of the soul, obstinate impenitence.

TWELFTH SUNDAY AFTER PENTECOST

The Sin of Slander

When our blessed Lord was on one occasion telling His disciples that they were especially favored since they had beheld wonders that princes and kings had long desired to behold, a certain lawyer who happened to be in the crowd, tempting him, said: "Master, what must I do to possess eternal life?" Apparently this man did not ask his question with a sincere heart, nevertheless our Lord deigned to reply. And from the answer given we learn that it is not sufficient to love God alone; we must also love our neighbor as ourselves.

The love of our neighbor, my children, demands that we should avoid everything that might injure him; particularly, we should never rob another of his good name. Imputing faults to our neighbor, denying his good qualities, exaggerating his trifling imperfections—all this constitutes the sin of slander, a sin that we must eradicate from our lives if we hope to observe God's holy law.

It is told of the famous Cardinal Lavigerie that he once returned to France to revisit his old home, but as a number of years had elapsed since he left his native country, and as he had changed considerably in appearance, it happened that for a time he passed unrecognized.

While he was waiting at a certain railway station in his old diocese, a man thus accosted him: "You are a missionary, I presume?" "I came from Algiers," was the brief reply. "Then you know our former bishop, Cardinal Lavigerie?" The cardinal assented. "How does he act now? Is he as queer as ever?" persisted his inquisitor. "Since he has been exposed to the hot African clime, I must confess that he is worse than ever," returned the cardinal. Thereupon the man launched forth into a harrowing discourse, enumerating not only possible trifling faults of the worthy prelate, but also many imaginary ones. When the train stopped at the little station, both cardinal and critic entered the same compartment, as they were going in the same direction. But all the time they were together the good bishop's travelling companion had nothing but abuse to bestow on the person in question.

When the man reached his destination, the cardinal, handing him his card, thus addressed him: "My friend, some of the qualities you have ascribed to me may be true, but by far the greater number are false." Seeing the name of his former bishop on the card presented him, the calumniator, struck dumb with confusion, hurried from the train.

Those who are addicted to slander, my children, have usually lost all sense of honor. In a word they are cowards; for if one tells you to your face of deeds you have committed, of faults of which you may have been guilty, you can defend yourself; but the slanderer says these things behind your back when you have no means of justification. He is like a cowardly murderer who stabs his enemy in the dark without giving any warning.

While several gentlemen were one day dining with a bishop, one of the guests opened a slanderous conversation about an absent person. In order to silence the calumniator, the prelate, calling one of his servants, ordered him to go and bring the gentleman whose character had been attacked. Immediately the slanderer begged his host to revoke the order, and not another word of detraction escaped his lips.

Among the many sins of injustice which are daily committed,

my children, there is none that weighs so heavily on the sinner's conscience as that of slander. As the thief must make restitution before his sin is forgiven, so also the calumniator must repair the damage done to his neighbor's character, and as this is sometimes almost impossible, regrets and remorse are the invariable result.

A woman once came to St. Philip Neri, and, acknowledging that she was much given to backbiting, she asked him to advise her how to rid herself of this fault. As she did not seem to realize that she was guilty of serious wrong, the saint endeavored to show her the extent of the evil by the following ingenious device. He said to her: "My daughter, do this as a penance. Go to the market and buy a chicken with its feathers still unpicked. As you pass along the streets, pluck out the feathers one by one and scatter them to the winds. Then come back to me."

Though marvelling at the strange advice, the woman nevertheless did as she was told. St. Philip, having praised her obedience, directed her to return by the same route as she had come, and collect all the feathers she had scattered. To this the good woman made answer: "Father, that is impossible for me to do, for the wind has carried them in all directions." Whereupon St. Philip replied: "And as widely as the wind disperses the feathers, just so far-reaching are the effects of slander. The persons hearing it go their several ways, carrying the news far and wide, till the evil is beyond recall."

Hence, my dear children, you see how detestable is the sin of slander, both in itself and in its results. If peace of conscience and your own salvation are dear to you, beware of this vice. Make the resolution now to say henceforth only what is good of your neighbor, or else to remain quiet. Jesus Christ Himself has promised: "This do, and thou shalt live."

THIRTEENTH SUNDAY AFTER PENTECOST

A Cancer of the Soul

Surely none of you, my dear children, like to be sick; none of you wish to be housed up in a dark room away from God's blessed sunshine, enduring perhaps agonizing pains. No, you want to be healthy and strong. And if you have had the ill fortune to have suffered from a wasting sickness, you long for the brightness of health to return to your eyes and the bloom of vigor to your cheeks.

In to-day's Gospel, my dear children, a pathetic sight meets our gaze. Ten men, afflicted with the loathsome disease of leprosy, seek our Lord's gentle touch for their cure. But it is not the healing of these poor sufferers to which I would call your attention; it is rather the malady itself I would have you consider. Leprosy is an incurable ailment, propagated by means of contact with the diseased person, and deemed so deadly that almost all nations have made laws concerning those infected. For instance, in our days they are banished from the general community to which they belong, and exiled to Molokai, the leper settlement, far away from communication with mankind.

But, direful as the leprosy of the body is, my children, it is not to be compared with the disease of the soul which it but faintly represents, the loathsome sin of impurity. As the suffering leper in the more advanced stages of his illness becomes a disgusting object even to his nearest and dearest, so the lewd person becomes an abomination in the sight of God. We should shun his society lest we too fall into the snare.

One day, Albini, a good pious child, was in the company of two or three boys of the same age as himself. At first they were amusing themselves very innocently, but during a lull in their games, one of the boys began to use bad words. Albini, noticing the drift of the conversation, immediately turned on the offender, with the rebuke: "Stop at once. Such words are not for you to utter, nor for us to hear." Encouraged by his dissolute companions, however, the other boy only laughed at his virtuous mentor, and continued to speak in the same strain as before. "Since you're determined to continue offending God," said the holy child, "I must leave you, for I can not remain here listening to words which may kill my soul." With this he departed from the group, followed by another boy, who, though too timid to chide the offender, nevertheless admired the courage of his youthful companion.

This child should be a model for you, my dear boys and girls, for the unclean tongue is an evil against which you should be on your guard. How frequently, as you pass along the street, do you not hear words and sentiments capable of sullying your purity? Perhaps your guardian angels are often compelled to turn away in sorrow as you stop on your way to hear the loose remark, the ribald jest.

But, you will say, such conversation can never have any effect on my mind or heart. My children, as you can not come in contact with fire without being burned, so you can not hearken to immodest words without having your purity tarnished more or less. Do you see that slender green vine creeping so prettily along the sides of yonder rock? So attractive does it look that you are tempted to pluck one of its glossy leaves. For a moment you are pleased with your treasure, but wait! A painful swelling shows itself on your little hand, and you cry out in distress: "Oh! I am poisoned!" Moral infection acts in much the same way, my children. Be cautious, therefore, to keep your hearts free from its withering blight.

It was a custom among the Jews that lepers must not come within the city limits lest they spread the dread contagion. Outside the city walls huts or hovels served for their abode, though oftener, perhaps, they had no place to lay their heads. If it was their lot to meet anyone not afflicted like themselves, they were forced to call out, "Unclean! Unclean!" Imagine if you can, my dear children, the anguish of such a heart-piercing cry, the pathos of such a fate, separated from all they held most dear. Yet how fortunate would it be if the evil speaker could be treated with a like isolation, if the unclean who are ever voicing vile words and lewd jests could be relegated to an island far removed from human kind, that other hearts might not be infected.

Pontentiana was a slave in the house of a pagan notorious for his evil life. Wicked as he was, he tried on several occasions to seduce this beautiful girl. At last, unsuccessful in his dastardly attempt, he denounced her to the governor as a Christian. The pious virgin, having been brought before the judge, was most cruelly tortured, but she remained steadfast in her purpose. Then the tyrant ordered a large caldron of boiling pitch to be prepared, that she might be cast into it. "Obey the will of your master," he commanded her, "or I will have you lowered into that seething liquid." "Until now," replied the innocent virgin, "I did not know that there existed a man capable of speaking such words of iniquity." Angered by her response, the judge forthwith ordered her to be consigned to the torture, but her only request was: "Lower me into the caldron little by little. My Lord Jesus, whom you know not, will strengthen me." For the space of three hours was she held immersed in the boiling pitch, yet no word of complaint escaped her, sustained as she was by the power of her Heavenly Spouse.

Such an example, my children, ought to spur you on to suffer any torment whatsoever rather than consent to a sin of impurity. The paltry tinsels of a tempting world should never lure you to sully that white garment of innocence you received at your baptism. Spotless you became, when the regenerating waters of the font were poured upon your infant brow; oh! thrice blessed will you be if spotless you return to the outstretched arms of your Maker!

FOURTEENTH SUNDAY AFTER PENTECOST

Seek First the Kingdom of God

"No man can serve two masters; for either he will hate the one and love the other, or he will sustain the one and despise the other."

How infallibly true, my children, are these blessed words, falling from the lips of our Divine Lord Himself! You can not serve God and the world. To render complete submission to two opposing sovereigns is not in the power of man. Why not then, while you are still young, take your oath of allegiance to the All Holy, lest time and circumstances should lure you to form an alliance with the world? On your choice will depend the right ordering of your life, the hope of a blissful eternity.

A great king of the East was once at the point of death. Sending for his trusted servant, he directed him to take his winding-sheet and, having suspended it on a pole, to go through the streets of his capital, crying: "Stop and look, ye passers-by! This winding-sheet is all the great Saladin will carry with him to the world beyond the grave!" We know not what effect the strange message had on the hearts of those who heard; only this we know, that as the king amid the splendors of his royal court had served no better master than the world, he could look for no reward. Shall we not learn from this to pledge our allegiance once for all to the eternal, everlasting God?

The story is told of a certain rich man who, having surrendered himself body and soul to the fleeting pleasures of the world, deemed himself the happiest of men. One day he sat, as was his wont, whiling away his hours in ease and opulence, and musing thus with himself: "Am I not the happiest of mortals? A large fortune is mine, good health and friends innumerable. But one thing troubles me: I must die! Death alone can sever me from all I love. And after death? What does my faith teach me?" The salutary words of Holy Scripture flashed before his mind, and particularly the answer of Abraham to the rich man in hell: "Son, remember that thou didst receive good things in thy lifetime, but now thou art tormented," and he mused: "This, then, is what I must expect in the life to come. Ah! it is better to live in this world like the beggar, Lazarus, than to share the fate of the rich man in eternity. My God, teach me how to live aright!" His meditation and prayer did not prove futile. From that hour a truly Christian spirit took possession of his heart; he shared his goods with the poor, cared no more for the vain joys of the world, and thus merited for himself the everlasting rewards of heaven.

While the saints were on earth, their only thought was the kingdom of heaven, their only anxiety the means of obtaining it. Let us do likewise. What is all the glamor of the world if we lose our immortal souls?

When the blessed Bernard filled the office of sacristan in the convent of Santarem, two little boys were accustomed to go there daily to be instructed in the principles of their holy religion. While in the convent, the children were allowed to enter the small chapel, and there, not far from the high altar, they studied their lessons and ate their lunch. Attracted by the image of Mary holding Jesus in her arms, they one day addressed the Infant in all simplicity: "Dear holy Child, how is it that you always remain in Your blessed Mother's arms? We will give you a share of our lunch if you but come down to us." As a reward of their childlike faith in Him, the Divine Child did leave His holy Mother's arms, and descended to the boys on the altar steps. So excessive became the love of Jesus in their hearts, that they cared for nothing but Him. Their parents, seeing the change wrought in the minds of their children, asked the reason of it, whereupon the little ones revealed to them their wonderful story. On Ascension Day, blessed Bernard's two little pupils served his Mass and received holy Communion from his saintly hands. The Sacrifice being completed, he knelt with his little servers upon the altar steps, and commended his soul to God. Great was the astonishment of some of the brothers, about an hour afterwards, to find the three, still in their reverential attitude, dead at the foot of the altar, and the heavenly smile on their beautiful faces told that they had gone home forever to the Divine Child.

My little boys and girls, like these good children, keep your souls free from the taint of sin and the Christ-Child will come to you too at the hour of your death. Be not solicitous about the things of the world. Your Father in heaven knows of what you stand in need, and He will supply the deficiency if you but cast your care upon Him. "Seek ye. therefore, first the kingdom of God and His justice, and all these things shall be added unto you."

FIFTEENTH SUNDAY AFTER PENTECOST

Homeward Bound

In this life, my dear children, we tread the weary mazes of this world, ever looking forward to the goal—the light on the other side of the distant hills; hand-in-hand we plod onward, each one of us living our little life, till the great day when time for us shall be no more. Widely separated though the paths may be on this side of the grave, still we are all making for the same resting place—heaven! And so when a little child dies, our loving Mother, the Church, whispers to the sorrowing friends: "Weep not! Your dear one has only gone before us to our heavenly home!" It was this thought that made St. Paul the Apostle exclaim, "O Grave, where is thy victory? O Death, where is thy sting?" Aye, verily, death is merely a step from time to eternity; why, then, should it make us sorrowful? Why should we mourn for those that are lost to us now, but not lost forevermore?

To the saints, death seemed ever a welcome event. Only by entering that portal, they knew, could they merit the face-to-face vision of their Lord. And why did they not fear the pangs and agonies of that final moment when the body severs its connection for a time from the soul? The only thing that makes death fearful, my dear children, is mortal sin; and, since the saints ever kept their souls undefiled in God's sight, they were able to face the closing scene of this mortal existence without flinching. Thus let it be with us. If sin is unknown in our little world, death will be only God's messenger to open for us the gates of life eternal.

When St. Francis Borgia was a young man at the court of the

Empress Isabella of Spain, he delighted in the plaudits and adulation of the world. Honor and fame seemed the keynote of his life. Gay, handsome and fascinating, he succeeded in winning an enviable position both in court circles and in the social whirl. But God did not allow him to barter his salvation for perishable things. Soon there came a lesson to his soul, taught by the Divine Preceptor Himself.

It happened that when he was Duke of Gandia his loved and esteemed empress died, and Francis was chosen to accompany her remains to the place of interment, as he had been numbered among her dearest friends. When the funeral cortege reached the royal burial place at Granada, the coffin was opened that the body might be identified. So repulsive was the sight that met the eyes of the beholders that they turned away in horror; that face, so lately the admiration of all Europe, was already a prey to the ravages of the tomb. On none did the dreadful spectacle make a more lasting effect than on the gay young Francis. When asked to verify the remains, he merely said: "Yes, this is indeed the body of Isabella," but then, overcome with emotion, he thus addressed his dead sovereign: "Can this be you, O my beautiful queen? What has become of those eyes, once sparkling with the light and brilliancy of youth? Ah! what has become of all your beauty, the admiration of your people and your nation?" On his return home Francis passed a restless night, the result of the harrowing scene he had so lately witnessed. Deep were his meditations on the vanity of human wisdom, and soon there was learned by his soul the lesson the Divine Master had come to teach: "True wisdom tells me to live only for God." The soul was won, the sacrifice complete. From that hour Francis forsook the world and led henceforth the life of a saint.

My children, it is well for you to learn that death is no respecter of persons. Young and old, rich and poor, king and peasant, must all alike be obedient to that final summons that echoes beyond the grave. Nor will time or place be of any protection to you; by night or day, on land or sea, the thread of life may be cut, and then woe to you if you are found unprepared. "You know not the day nor the hour," are our blessed Lord's own words.

In the reign of Henry VIII. of England there lived a man notorious for his frivolous life and many crimes. The blessed Thomas More, having visited him on one occasion, begged him to change his evil life and do penance. "Oh! don't be alarmed about me," replied the hardened sinner. "I shall one day repent. There are three little words that shall act as a talisman for me at the last— 'Lord, pardon me.'" "Ah! my friend," answered blessed Thomas, "take care. You may still lose your soul." But the advice was lost on the unfortunate man; he continued to live in sin as before.

Not long afterwards, it happened that, being on horseback, he had occasion to cross a bridge that spanned a deep river. A mere trifle caused the horse to start, and with one wild bound the animal jumped with its luckless rider over the parapet into the river. The onlookers heard his words, "May the devil—," but the curse died on the lips that uttered it, for the unhappy man was never seen alive again. Such, my children, is the risk of relying on a deathbed conversion.

We should learn early in life, my children, to provide for ourselves treasures beyond the grave. Let us not trust to the suffrages of others when our eyes are closed in death. Once the sod is placed over our mortal remains, we are soon forgotten. The tears that fall so freely on the day of our burial will speedily be dried, the sorrowing heart comforted, and we will be but a memory even to our dearest friends. It behooves us then to work while we have yet time. Let us lead lives of such purity and goodness that when death comes to summon us from the midst of our loved ones, we will answer his call not with tears and trembling, but with a trustful smile and a clear conscience. May our last words be: "My Lord Jesus, call me to dwell with You in the home of the blessed of Your Father!"

SIXTEENTH SUNDAY AFTER PENTECOST

Sanctifying the Lord's Day

In six days Almighty God created the world, according to the teachings of Holy Scripture, and on the seventh He rested. Now why, my children, did the Most High put it into the mind of the inspired writer to tell us of this day of rest? To show us that we, too, need to set aside a day of repose, a day of contemplation and recollection, that our hearts may not become too enamored of the things of this world. "Remember thou keep holy the Sabbath day," says the little catechism that teaches us the principles of the religion of Christ. But how do many of our young people sanctify Sundays and holy days? By hearing Mass? Not so. It is an unfortunate truth that a large number of Catholics are Catholic only in name, since they disregard entirely the Commandments of God and His Church. Instead of sanctifying the Lord's Day, by assisting at Mass and attending other religious devotions, they while away their time in sensual enjoyments and worldly pleasures. Alas for them, that they forget, "Now is the acceptable time; now is the day of salvation!"

The severest punishments of God are often meted out to those unhappy souls, who thus neglect the precepts of our holy Mother the Church. It is related that certain tradesmen of Gubic had on one occasion gone to a public fair held in the town of Cisterno. When all their merchandise had been disposed of, two of them began to make arrangements for returning home: they planned to set out at dawn on the morrow, a Sunday. But a third one objected to this, saying that he did not wish to start on the homeward journey without first being present at the Sacrifice of the Altar. He added, however: "That will not delay us much. We can hear Mass early in the morning, and after a slight repast take our departure." His companions, not wishing their plans upset, would not agree to this. "Almighty God," they argued, "will not punish us if we omit Mass just this once." So the next morning at the first break of dawn they departed, leaving their comrade to follow them later.

In course of time the eager travelers reached the river Corfun, which a heavy rain of the previous night had swollen to such a degree that its angry waters flowed like a raging tide. No sooner had the unfortunate men gained the middle of the bridge that spanned the stream, when the entire structure gave way, consigning the unhappy traders to a watery grave. At the sound of the terrific crash the villagers ran excitedly from all directions, eager to render assistance to those whose lives were endangered, but their efforts were of no avail. All they could do was recover the bodies of the lost. Soon afterwards the third tradesman reached the river. Seeing the crowd of people standing on its banks, he joined them only to recognize the mortal remains of his two companions lying side by side. When he heard the sad story he knelt and returned thanks to God for having saved him from a like fate. To his dying day he remembered it was the holy Sacrifice of the Altar that had been his preservation.

The Mass, my dear children, is the source of many blessings to those who assist devoutly at its celebration. For the sinner it merits the grace of repentance; for the just, that of perseverance. Not unfrequently, also, it bestows remarkable temporal favors on the needy.

How sublime then, my children, how all-sufficient must not the holy Sacrifice of the Altar be, that merits such a reward. God asks of us this favor but once a week: "Come to My House of Prayer at least for half an hour on Sunday morning. I have many good things in store for you. Will you refuse them?" Yet in spite of pressing invitations and repeated promises, how many with reckless indifference do not remain away? Be not like the guests whom the king invited to his son's marriage feast: "And they would not come." The moments of the Mass are the most precious ones of the whole week. Why, then, should we slight them? In that short space Jesus sits enthroned on the altar, His heart burning with ardent desire to soothe our sorrows, calm our sighs. How wounded and heartsore must He not feel when we reject His invitation and heed Him not.

It is said that blessed John Berchmans when he first went to school at the age of seven, was observed day after day leaving home very early. On being questioned, the holy boy acknowledged that he attended several Masses every morning in order to bring the blessing of God upon his school life. He was a mere child, younger than many of you, my children, and see what he did. Is there any excuse for us then? Like the sea-tossed mariner who often must steer into the harbor to have the stock of his ship replenished, so, too, must we seek the haven of the House of God, that by the holy Sacrifice of the Mass we may gain renewed strength to cope with the fierce assaults of temptation.

SEVENTEENTH SUNDAY AFTER PENTECOST

On Intimate Terms with God

"Thou shalt love the Lord thy God with thy whole heart, and with thy whole soul, and with thy whole mind." This is the greatest and the First Commandment.

Have you ever tried, my dear children, to learn the significance of this "greatest and First Commandment," as God wishes you to learn it? What does it mean? In simple language, it means to be on intimate terms with God. The youngest of you gathered here knows what it is to love your parents: You want to be always with them; you long to see your gentle mother's face looking down on you when you open your eyes at the break of day; you wish to be the first to greet father when he wearily plods his way homeward after a hard day's work; you twine your little arms about their necks, look up into their tender eyes, and draw their faces down to yours for a kiss. And these are some of the outward marks of love, my children, that you exhibit towards your parents; it is being united on terms of the warmest intimacy with those who take God's place in your regard. Now, how are we to be in close relation with God Himself? How are we to love Him? With our whole heart, with our whole soul, and with all our mind. When the little eyelids open in the morning, and the little body is clothed for the day, then you should kneel down and give your morning greeting to God; when the little head is aching and you don't know what to do because of the pain, an aspiration to Jesus in the Tabernacle, a thought of all He endured for us, may help you to bear this slight suffering for love of Him; when the little eyes won't stay open more than a minute longer, a look at Jesus, a last thought for Him, will coax Him to watch tenderly over you during the night. And that means loving Jesus; letting Him pass judgment on our little cares and sorrows, and sharing with Him our joys. This is giving our whole heart to Him. Can not all of you do this, my children?

St. Ephrem used to cry out, "Lord, retire for a little while; my weak nature cannot endure such love"; and St. Francis Xavier exclaimed, "Lord, it is enough!" Why were the saints filled with such rapture that they would fain withdraw from the consolations of God? Because having surrendered themselves to Him with all their hearts, they had thereby obtained a foretaste of heaven. No matter in what condition of life we are placed, we too may win for ourselves a like reward if we model our lives on the angelic lives of God's own saints.

In the desert of the Thebaid there lived a holy man named Paphnutius, the most perfect of all the hermits who dwelt there. Hour by hour and day by day he strove to advance in perfection, that he might thus make himself more acceptable to God. One day he prayed with fervent supplication that if there was anyone then near more perfect than himself, God should enlighten his mind and show him where the holy man was, that he might seek him and learn more of the principles of sanctity. The Almighty heard his prayer and directed him to go to a certain city where he would find the one most acceptable to the heart of God. Betaking himself thither, Paphnutius saw in the market place a poor man playing a street organ, surrounded by a jolly, dancing crowd. Immediately an interior voice seemed to whisper that the street musician was the man he sought. When an opportunity presented itself, Paphnutius inquired of him: "My good man, tell me in what way do you serve God?" to which the other replied, "Father, I am a very great sinner. Years ago I was a robber by trade, but, by the grace of God I repented of my crimes, and now I am trying to make reparation for my past life." Marvelling at the answer he had received, the saint returned to his desert home, blessing God, Who in His abounding mercy gave to the poor people of the world means to become as perfect as the monk in his monastery.

Perhaps you have often wondered, my children, how the martyrs in the first ages of the Church, and even at the present day in pagan countries, exhibit such wonderful cheerfulness despite the dreadful tortures to which they are subjected. The reason is, they have passed their lives in the sunlight of God's grace. See the soft, radiant smile on their features, the bright, beaming look in their eyes, and you will not need to be told that they possess the key to true happiness, the life-giving grace of the Almighty. The more He reigns in our soul, the more peace and happiness will be ours. The less we give Him of our heart's affection, the less contentment will we enjoy either here or hereafter.

It is related of a little boy in Brittany that he was accustomed to row across a nearby river to hear Mass on Sunday, in the only church that was accessible to the country people. With the greatest fervor he attended the holy Sacrifice, and received our dear Lord in the Sacrament of His love. Then when his thanksgiving was over, he would linger by the altar-railing, as though loathe to go. Finally, when the clock struck the hour of departure, he would lovingly throw a kiss of farewell to the Tabernacle door and say: "Good-bye, dear Lord, but only for a little while. Sunday will soon be here again." And with a parting sigh he was off, strengthened to bear his trials for another week.

Would you doubt for a moment, my dear children, that that brave little heart was on intimate terms with God? Surely, the Divine Tenant of the Tabernacle guided his every step, because of his childlike absolute trust. Oh! if we were at all like him, we would realize only too fully the meaning of the words of holy Scripture, "Taste and see that the Lord is sweet." This world would no longer be for us a "vale of tears," but the outer court of Paradise.

EIGHTEENTH SUNDAY AFTER PENTECOST

The Interest of Our Lord Paramount

My Dear Children:—How tender is the Divine Heart of Jesus! A suffering man is brought to Him, and, without a word, He heals him because of the faith of these simple people. But let us see whether in working miracles our Lord restores to health the afflicted body without any regard for the wounded soul. Rather His custom is to say first: "Thy sins are forgiven thee," and then only to bring about the restoration of the diseased members. Is the soul then really more precious than the body? Oh! infinitely more so, my children. There can hardly be a comparison between the two. The soul is the priceless gem for which our Lord suffered and died. The poor, worn body may decay; the marble tombstone that marks its resting-place may crumble to pieces; but the soul, in a state of blissful reward or direful punishment, shall live forever. For these reasons it is the soul that should be the object of paramount importance to us, not the frail body that perishes with death.

Though we may learn a beneficial lesson from the gentle care exhibited by the poor people in bringing this palsied man to our Lord, yet there is a greater lesson taught us than caring for the sickly body of our neighbor—we ought particularly to consider the interests of the soul. If you know of persons who neglect to hear Mass on Sundays, who are strangers to the life-giving Sacraments, you should feel that God is calling you to be little Apostles in their regard. A kind word, a gentle explanation, may dispel all difficulties and you may be the means of performing the greatest of all acts of charity—bringing erring, wayward souls back to God.

There was once an old army officer who had passed his whole life in neglect of his religious duties. One day, on being informed that a mission was being given by a certain great preacher in the town where he was then stationed, he resolved to attend some of the sermons. Entering the church one evening, he found the priest discoursing on the necessity of making a good confession, and the interior peace experienced by the devout penitent after such an expiation of sin. The officer, while listening to the eloquent words of the holy preacher, realized his own spiritual condition and the hazardous position in which he was placing himself. Disturbed in mind, he sought the missionary after the sermon was ended and said: "Father, I wish to speak to you. I want to make my peace with God, for at present I am far from happy." There and then he made his confession with the greatest sorrow and compunction of heart. According to his own words, he felt as though a heavy burden had been lifted from his shoulders, and it was with tears in his eyes that he listened to the long-deferred absolution being pronounced over his penitent heart. Afterwards he exclaimed in an ecstasy of joy: "O my God, I never could have imagined that anyone could feel so happy. This is indeed the happiest day of my life."

Rejoining his companions he declared that he had never enjoyed such peace as he had since he had become reconciled with his heavenly Father, and he advised them to do as he had done, that they too might taste the same joy. You see, my children, this old officer's charity bore the true stamp. As soon as he realized the heavenly blessing that had been conferred on him he wished to share it with his comrades. After that nothing pleased him more than to see one of his friends reconciled to his God.

When we are attacked by a serious illness, our first care ought to be the healing of our soul. Though disease is not always a direct punishment of sin, it is nevertheless sent at times by an all-merciful Father to bring about a change in our sinful mode of life. Therefore let us have in the first place oil and wine poured into the wounds of our soul, and the frail body may soon rejoice in its cure.

Doctor Tissot, a French physician renowned for his extraordinary skill, was one day called to attend a Catholic young woman who was stricken with a dangerous sickness. When he made known to his patient that her case was well-nigh hopeless, she became despondent at the thought of leaving the world so young. The doctor, though a non-Catholic, immediately told her friends to send for a priest that he might administer to her the last rites of religion.

When the clergyman reached the bed of the dying girl, he endeavored by kind words and holy sentiments to prepare her soul for its last journey. Soon a peaceful calm came over the wasted features, and she received the Sacraments with the greatest edification to all present.

Next morning the doctor again called, only to find that the sufferer had undergone a marvellous change: the fever had diminished, and the most alarming symptoms of the disease had disappeared. In a short time she was on the road to recovery. In terms of the greatest reverence Doctor Tissot ever afterwards recalled this event of which he had been a personal witness, and from that time on he entertained sincere veneration for the Sacrament of the Catholic Church.

If I were to ask you to-day, my children, to which you give the most attention, your soul or your body, I am afraid you would have to answer to the latter; and yet that is not according to God's ordering. Every little ache your body endures you try to cure, but the ills of your soul are neglected. Daily you feed and adorn your frail body. What care do you bestow on your soul? Does it not languish for the food of prayer, and you do not supply its want? Does it not thirst for the cleansing graces of the Sacrament, and you are careless of its need? Oh! my children, your soul should be everything to you, rather than your body. If you have ever looked on a body from which the soul has fled, you can not help but realize this. Those eyes that danced with the brilliancy of life are now sightless; those lips that moved in mirth and song are silent; those hands that busied themselves with deeds of kindness are at rest; and above all that heart that loved you, that throbbed for you only, perhaps, is still and cold.

And so will your bodies be, my dear little ones, when the soul, the breath of God, has forsaken its earthly habitation. Learn, then, to make your body the servant of your soul; learn not to be overanxious about what you shall eat nor wherewith you shall be clothed, for after these things the heathen seek, but do you seek first the kingdom of God. When you say your night prayers as this old earth of ours is mantling for sleep and rest, ask yourself: "What have I done to-day for my body, and what for my soul?" May the answer always be: "Not alone, dear Lord, have I sought the comforts of this poor flesh of mine. To-day at least I have endeavored to gain Thine grace and love!"

NINETEENTH SUNDAY AFTER PENTECOST

THE ROYAL BANQUET HALL OF GOD

"The kingdom of heaven is likened to a king who made a marriage for his son."

These words of to-day's Gospel, my dear children, form the opening sentence of another of those many parables spoken by our Divine Lord to the Jewish priests and Pharisees, and, like all the sentiments uttered by Jesus Christ, they have a mystic meaning that it is well for us to fully understand. The king is the Eternal Father, the Ruler of the universe; the son is Jesus Christ, true God and true man; and the marriage feast is prepared in a right royal banquet hall, the Church, where a regal repast is served for the invited guests.

"And he sent his servants, to call them that were invited to the marriage, and they would not come." That is the sad part, my children, when our good Lord Jesus, a Prisoner of Love here on earth, has to acknowledge that His own, His beloved, will not answer His call. Way back in the ages the Gentiles refused to obey His law; then came the era when the Jews, His chosen people, His own nation, received Him not; and now, how many of us does not that ever-patient Lord invite to His inner court, His holy place, and—we reject His invitation!

The great Fenelon, Bishop of Cambrai, was so renowned for his signal piety and illustrious virtues that those who visited him were forced to acknowledge: "The Church to which that good Bishop belongs must indeed be the Church of God, since none other could produce such a man." On one occasion Lord Peterborough, a nobleman of Fenelon's time, hearing of his eminent merits, resolved to seek an interview with him. The saintly prelate received his visitor with every mark of honor and respect, and so extraordinary was the impression created that the nobleman was heard to remark: "I can not remain here any longer, for if I do, I shall become a Catholic even in spite of myself."

Would to God that our example, my children, was such that it would produce wonders like this! And why should we not become as virtuous as the celebrated Fenelon? Perhaps our Lord lavishes on us even greater blessings than He bestowed on him. We have the same Sacred Food as he had, Jesus Christ whole and entire in the Sacrament of His love, the same Divine example upholds us, the same holy Sacrifice is perpetually offered for us, the same faith, the same law, the same Sacraments. What more does our need require? Oh! let us resolve to make good use of the ample means that have been placed within our reach, and nothing can prevent us from growing ever more holy and pleasing to God.

But certain ones have been called by our blessed Lord to occupy a higher position in His Church, namely, priests and bishops. They are His chosen servants, His devout followers, His self-sacrificing ministers whose sacred duty it is to officiate at His holy altar. It is the priest who places our Lord Jesus Christ in the Tabernacle, who pours the cleansing waters over our souls in baptism, who gives us holy Viaticum at the last, and anoints our bodies with the sacred chrism. His touch is the first to free us from the bonds of sin when we enter into life, the last to ease the pain and suffering, when our life in this sinful world is at an end. It is through him we receive every blessing, from him we obtain our passport to life eternal. Oh! how we should then revere the priest, who having been duly ordained by his lawful bishop, has been sent forth to preach the Gospel, an heir to all the privileges bestowed by our Lord Himself on His first Apostles. Yet this Church, instituted by our Lord Jesus Christ, is not to be free from persecutions. No, the servant can not fare better than his lord and master. But despite the sufferings inflicted upon it both from traitors within and deserters without, it shall nevertheless pass unscathed through its trials. Upheld by the strong arm of God, it shall be ever victorious in the battles it must needs wage.

From the caverned rocks of St. Helena, the great Napoleon, now an exile, was once gazing over the troubled deep. Sea, earth and sky alike claimed his attention as he reviewed in his mind the empires of the world, at one time boasting of an enviable place among the nations, but soon crumbling to the dust from whence they came. Then, having considered the fate of great men, how to-day they are the idols of the hour, and to-morrow they are no more, he suddenly exclaimed: "The nations of the earth pass away, the thrones of world-wide kingdoms fall to the ground, and the Church of God alone remains."

That was the judgment of a man who had had the sway over more than one great realm. He saw the nations come and go, but God's Church remained intact. Ever since her humble beginning in the upper chamber at Jerusalem the world has admired the Catholic Church. The greatest minds have pointed her out as the grandest institution of the centuries, and yet there are some men so cowardly, so craven, that they are ashamed to be called Catholics. They would fain withhold their allegiance or else become traitors in the camp.

There was once a minister of state in Holland, who, though a Protestant, had the greatest esteem for the Catholic belief, and would place no trust in those who denied their religion. On one occasion a young man came to him soliciting employment in the service of the government. "To what religion do you belong?" questioned the minister. "I am a Catholic," was the ready response, "but I do not care much whether I continue to be one or not." "Then I have no appointment for you," replied the statesman. "You were born and brought up in the greatest institution in the world, and yet you betray your cause! A Catholic who does not love and esteem his faith as his greatest treasure is not fit for the king's service, since he knows not how to serve his God."

Thoroughly abashed by the stern reproof, the young man would willingly have retracted his statement, but it was too late. The minister having said these words, dismissed him.

What a glorious privilege then, my dear boys and girls, has God bestowed on you in making you the children of His one true Church. Therefore esteem your holy faith as a priceless treasure, and never be ashamed of it, since it carries with it manifold blessings. Let not the judgment of Almighty God, that those that were invited were not worthy, be passed on you. Rather may you be numbered among those chosen souls who, clothed in the wedding garment of innocence, frequent the banquet hall of holy Church till the passing things of life be changed to the realties of eternity.

TWENTIETH SUNDAY AFTER PENTECOST

The Gift of Faith

My Dear Children:—We have more than ample proof from the many wonderful cures wrought by the Divine Physician, Jesus of Nazareth, that these good people of Judea believed implicitly in His miraculous power, else the marvelous wonders would never have taken place. Yet occasionally we find those gentle lips pronouncing a tender rebuke when faith was in any way defective. And in this chapter from St. John, treating of the healing of the ruler's son of Capharnaum, there seems to have been something wanting, for we hear Jesus saying: "Unless you see signs and wonders, you believe not." How often can not our gentle Saviour reprove us in similar words! How often do not we, too, poor and weak and miserable as we are, claim for ourselves a degree of superiority, and dictate terms to our Lord and Master! If we examine the world to-day, we shall find many so-called Christians believing not what the Son of God taught, but what their own weak intellects suggest. They do not want to believe in a hell, so they affirm that an all-merciful God could not prepare such a place of torment. They forget that He is an all-just God as well, and that nothing defiled can enter the kingdom of heaven. To such people one religion is as good as another, but, my children, these are the "false prophets," of whom Christ Himself told us to beware. Therefore, flee the company of such Christians. If in doubt about any of the great mysteries of your religion, consult your catechism. The truths written there are unchangeable. It is only by knowing your religion well, and reverencing its doctrines that you can hope to retain that precious gift of faith bestowed on you, though so undeserving of it.

Many years ago a Catholic young man entered the army of a Persian Shah, and, so exemplary was his conduct, that he soon gained the affection and esteem of his sovereign. Only one thing seemed to be a barrier in the way of their affection—their difference in religious views. One day the Shah, calling the young man to him, entreated him to renounce the Christian religion, adding: "If you will do this, I assure you I will raise you to the highest rank the army can offer." "My king," replied the youth, "my father died for you, and I am ready to do the same, but, renounce my religion—never! Rather take this sword and drain with it my heart's warm blood, for a thousand deaths are preferable to me than to be guilty of such a crime." Moved by these steadfast words, the Shah, instead of being angry, praised the young Christian, and as a mark of esteem conferred on him the highest honors of the Persian army.

Doubtless you have sometimes heard, my children, that in the olden days human beings were often sold as slaves to whatever masters chanced to buy them. As cattle pass from one owner to another, so were these poor souls traded by their owners. Such a condition of affairs seems the limit of cruelty, yet, has it never occurred to you that all the little souls here assembled before me were once slaves? You look surprised, but it is true, my children. Yes, every one of you were slaves under the dominion of the tyrannical master, Lucifer. He had stolen you from your lawful inheritance, the kingdom of heaven, but you were still very dear to Jesus, the Son of God. He could not bear the thought of His little children being in the miserable condition of serfdom, so He came down from His bright, beautiful heaven to our poor, miserable earth. Thus did He repurchase for you your inheritance; thus did He once more adorn your soul with the precious gift of faith. You have done nothing to merit this consideration of your Saviour, yet since faith has once been conferred upon you, you should put forth your best endeavors to retain the priceless boon. Be not indifferent to your religion, whatever the circumstance, and do not associate with those who would fain make you believe that all churches are alike. Avoid the company of those also who make a practice to ridicule everything that is holy.

There was once a prosperous farmer who, having an only son, took great pains to have him well instructed in his religion. Unhappily the boy was often obliged to go to a neighboring town, where he met among others certain so-called liberal-minded people who sneered at the very name of God and His Church. At first the boy ably defended his religious principles, but soon growing tired of the wrangling, he lapsed into silence, till as time went on he became as godless as the scoffers themselves. The father hearing of the bad company his son kept, called the boy to him and reproved him thus: "My son, have I not already warned you of the company you keep? If you do not once for all quit these licentious men, you will expose yourself to the danger of losing your faith. Have you forgotten your mother's last words to you: 'Keep God always before your eyes and shun irreligious company, that you may not lose your faith. Often look up to heaven, and live so as not to forfeit the place God has prepared for you there'!"

But the young man heeded not his father's advice. Angered by the reproof which he considered undeserved, he left his father's house, only to become more wicked than the worst of his boon companions. Not long after his father died of a broken heart. In less than two years the handsome fortune left to the boy had all been squandered. Years of dissipation succeeded each other, fateful years in which he went from bad to worse. At last he was brought to a hospital fatally ill. The priest who was called to his bedside urged him to make his peace with God. "Is your mother still alive?" he asked. No question could have touched the heart of the dying man more than this. "My good mother has been dead for years," he answered, "but what a disgrace I am to her! While I was leaning over her bed to catch her dying message, she gently murmured, 'Son, often look up to heaven and live so that you may not lose your place there.' Poor mother! Her advice was never heeded! Long ago did I lose the place God had destined for me!" "Do not say that," pleaded the priest. "The way of salvation is still open to you—make a good confession and God will forgive all."

Ere evening cast a veil of darkness over the weary hearts of earth, another soul, justified by penance, was clasped in the arms of its Maker.

But faith alone, without good works, is not sufficient for salvation, my children. Holy Scripture tells us: "Faith without good works is dead." It is like a body from which the spirit has departed. How can a man who knows that sin is the greatest evil on earth be said to have faith if he continues to live in sin? How can a boy, realizing that Jesus is ever present on the altar, be said to exercise faith if he behaves irreverently in the shadow of the sanctuary?

One day an Arab asked a Catholic whom he met and whose conduct was far from corresponding to the faith he professed, if he believed in God. "Of course I do," answered the man indignantly. "Did you ever hear of a Catholic who didn't?" "No," replied the Arab, "I did not; but as for you, you may indeed say with your lips that you believe in God, yet surely you will not deny that your actions belie your words."

So it is often with you also, my children. Examine your conduct from the time you arise in the morning till you go to sleep at night, and see if your actions correspond with your words. "Be not faithless but believing," is our blessed Lord's injunction to us. If we obey that Divine command, if we are Christians, followers of Christ, not only in name but in deed, can we doubt for an instant that the place reserved for us in heaven will once be ours?

TWENTY-FIRST SUNDAY AFTER PENTECOST

Forgiving Injuries

"And his lord being angry, delivered him to the torturers until he paid all the debt. So shall my heavenly Father do to you if you forgive not every one his brother from your hearts."

A sad record it is indeed, my dear children, that our Lord Jesus Christ has outlined for us in this striking parable, a record of base ingratitude and vindictiveness. And yet we see this same spirit exemplified daily in our own sinful lives. God forgives us great and frequent transgressions, and yet we refuse to pardon our neighbor who perhaps has spoken to us a trifle less kindly than usual. Are not we then as blameworthy as this servant who owed his lord ten thousand talents? This is not observing the precept of charity laid down for us by our Divine Saviour; this is not loving our neighbor as ourselves. And not only must we forgive our enemies from the bottom of our hearts, my children, we must do more than this: we must wish them well, and, above all, pray for them.

A poor negro by the name of Tom was once bought by some slave owners on the coast of Africa, and carried by them to the West Indies. In his new home he had the happiness of embracing the Christian religion. After his conversion he endeavored to lead a most holy life, and by bearing patiently all the hardships that fell to his lot he soon became a model of Christian perfection even to his master.

One day, the latter wishing to purchase a number of slaves for his plantation, asked the faithful Tom to accompany him. As they were examining the slaves in order to buy the most suitable, Tom saw in the market-place an old gray-haired man, whom he immediately recognized. Turning to his master, he begged him to purchase the old negro, but he received the abrupt answer: "No, indeed, Tom. What use will that old slave be to us? He can no longer do any work, and I am not wealthy enough to spend money on useless objects." The owner of the slave, however, hearing this response, forthwith offered him for nothing, provided Tom's master bought twenty other slaves. So the old man changed hands.

So singular was the regard of Tom for this newly-purchased slave that his master began to wonder at it. What could be the cause of his excessive devotion? Why did he offer the old gray-haired negro the use of his own cabin? Why did he seem to be ever on the watch for occasions to serve this particular slave? Again and again had these thoughts puzzled the master, till one day he could not refrain any longer from finding out the apparent mystery. Calling Tom to him, he asked: "Is that old man your father?" "No, Massa," answered Tom, with a merry twinkle in his eye. "Then he must be an uncle of yours, or some near relative," persisted the master. "You would surely never be so interested in an utter stranger. Tell me, who is he?" "That man," replied Tom, hesitating as he said each word, "is my bitter enemy. Long ago he stole me from my home and parents, and made me a slave. But— I can not hate him. The missionary told me that I must forgive my enemies and do good to those who have injured me. If my enemy is hungry, I must give him to eat; if thirsty, I must give him to drink. That is the reason why I have taken this old man under my special care."

Do you not admire the Christianity of this poor negro, my children? Who of us would do as much? Truly, those that are far below us in wealth and refinement often put us to shame when religion is in question. Let us then fulfill the command of our Divine Lord, wholly and entirely: "Do good to them that **hate** you and pray for them that persecute and calumniate you."

But some will say: "I can not forgive." That is simply **not true**, my children. Has God ever commanded anything that is impossible? "But," you persist, "my neighbor has offended me too grievously." And what do you call a grievous offence? Has he scourged you? Crowned you with thorns? Crucified you? And even if all these sufferings were inflicted upon you, it is your place to still cry out: "Father, forgive him, for he knows not what he does." Otherwise, how can you declare that you are a follower of Christ? Remember that the greater the injury done you, the more glorious will be the reward if you forgive your enemy from your heart.

Long years ago there lived in a hamlet in Spain a poor widow with her only son. Spending their lives in good deeds, they seemed all-sufficient for each other, content if God was pleased with their little round of duties. But an evening came when their joyous dream was brought to a sad end. Some young men of the town had taken part in a heated discussion over a trifling subject. A quarrel ensued, and one youth was killed. Vaguely had the reports come to the widow, but before she was made aware of all the frightful details a young man rushed into her home, his face pale, his clothes stained with blood. "My good woman," he cried, *"I* have done this cruel deed of which you have heard. They are pursuing me. For Christ's sake save me." A moment of hesitation, then she led the self-confessed murderer into an adjoining room, where she hid him from the justice of the law. Hardly had she done so when the pale corpse of her only son was brought to her house, but the brave woman did not flinch. No cry escaped her lips as they laid him on the very bed under which the murderer was hiding. A moment more and an officer entered, saying to her: "People say the culprit is here. Can it be true?" "How could you imagine such a thing?" replied the heartbroken mother, and the officer left the house, without a further word. As soon as everything was quiet and the shades of night wrapped the world in darkness, the poor mother sought the one whose hand had done the cruel deed. Giving him some of her boy's clothing that he might disguise himself, she nobly helped him to make good his escape, saying as a parting word: "May God forgive you as I have done. Go and do penance for your crime."

Was not that good mother a valiant woman, my children? How nobly did she not subdue all natural feeling and obey God's precept: "Do good to them that injure you." Oh! let us then pardon the little wrongs, the little slights that we may have to bear from others. Let us forgive our enemies gladly, remembering the words that God Himself put upon our lips: "Forgive us our trespasses as we forgive those who trespass against us." Only in this way can we hope for the remission of our many sins.

TWENTY-SECOND SUNDAY AFTER PENTECOST

GIVE TO GOD WHAT BELONGS TO GOD

"Render, therefore, to Caesar the things that are Caesar's, and to God the things that are God's."

You are all willing enough, my children, to render to Caesar the things that are Caesar's. You are willing to give to the world far more than its due need of honor and glory, but what about the concerns of God? Are you as anxious to surrender to Him what belongs to Him? Your heavenly Father has created you; in His boundless love He has preserved you to this very moment. And what return have you made? Earth, sea and sky send up their matin hymn of adoration; they obey His will—the will of God. Do you do as much? That little heart whose every pulsation ought to be a psalm of love to its Creator, where are its affections, its desires, its burning love? Only when you direct all your faculties to the honor and glory of God who made you, can you be said to be doing your share in giving Him what rightfully is His due.

This was the secret of the saints' success, my children—they gave themselves wholly and entirely to their heavenly Father. By this pious practice they acquired that ardent love of God, that generous zeal for His glory, that perfect purity of soul and body, that tender charity for their fellow men which distinguished them from all others, and contributed to make them saints.

That holy servant of God, St. Ignatius, devoted his life entirely to the love of Jesus Christ. Whatever he knew to be pleasing to Jesus, he did. Poverty and humiliations were joyfully suffered that he might become more like to Jesus. He ardently longed for others to join him in serving Jesus, and so he selected for the motto of his society: "All for the greater glory of God." No wonder that our blessed Lord promised him that the previous heritage of His Passion should never fail his community. Solicit, therefore, through St. Ignatius, my dear children, the grace ever to perform all your actions for the glory of God, no matter what sufferings it may entail. Every day of your life belongs to God; He has merely lent it to you to be employed in His Divine service. Not only must you begin the day well, but as the hours speed onward to eternity you should perfect what you have begun. In all things seek God's holy will, and thus make profitable that precious talent of time which He has entrusted to your care.

When St. Peter of Alcantara was still a child, he distinguished himself for his love of prayer and his spirit of recollection. He rose early in the morning that he might have time to make his meditation, which he often prolonged for many hours. Then, repairing to the church, he heard Mass with great devotion and frequently received holy Communion. Though he spent the rest of the day in school, he never forgot God. Even when walking along the street, his heart was continually raised to his Maker in a supplicating prayer for help or an ardent act of love. Truly, his conversation was in heaven.

At meals he always left a portion untouched on his plate, thus mortifying Himself for the love of God, while he never drank anything but water, though in those countries it is customary even for children to drink diluted wine. It happened one day when the dinner hour approached Peter was missing. In vain they searched the garden, the house—everywhere—Peter could not be found. At length they sought the oratory: There was the holy child on his knees, his hands clasped, his eyes raised in mute appeal to heaven.

No thought of the necessaries of life had entered his mind—he was alone with his God!

What a reproach is not the conduct of this holy child when contrasted with those boys and girls, who, so far from forgetting their meals through love for their prayers, often sit down to breakfast without having ever lifted their hearts to God, without having once thanked Him for the day begun.

Some time ago I noticed a little boy in earnest supplication before the Tabernacle. Doubtless he knew not that another person was kneeling there, enjoying, like Him, intimate communion with his God. Perhaps he thought that the bright light of the sanctuary lamp and his lonely little heart were all that were offering adoration to the silent Lord. His hands were clasped, his eyes raised to God. Moments elapsed without betraying any movement on the part of the lone child. Then a little girl, prettily dressed, gaily tripped up the aisle. Up, farther up she went, till she gained the dimly lighted sanctuary. On the spotless cloth she laid the offering she had come to bring—a bouquet of beautiful roses, and I doubt not her little heart spoke its pious greeting to the Prisoner of the Tabernacle. A dimpling smile to Jesus, and—she was gone. Again my eyes sought the devout face far down the aisle. "Dear Lord," he whispered, "I've no pretty flowers to give you. But listen: I have a heart that loves you. Take it, won't you, and keep it always!"

Which of these precious gifts, my children, do you think was the more pleasing to the Silent Listener there? Ah! some author has said: "Flowers are the sweetest things God ever made, and forgot to put a soul into." But what, think you, would that same author have written about the throbs of a dear little human heart?

"Render, therefore, to Caesar the things that are Caesar's, and to God the things that are God's." Could any words be plainer? How, then, can we refuse our Divine Lord the gifts that are so unmistakably His? Not one day only of our lives should we offer to His service, but rather the far-stretching years. Let each dawn find us ever pressing onward, each sunset nearer the "Great White Throne."

TWENTY-THIRD SUNDAY AFTER PENTECOST

Obstinacy in Sin

My Dear Children:—The sad image of a soul grown old in the ways of iniquity is presented to us in the afflicted woman mentioned in to-day's Gospel. How pathetic is her need, how evident her distress! Yet she thinks within herself: "If I shall touch only the hem of His garment, I shall be healed." What sublime faith in the all-healing power of God is hers? If only ours were like it, how much greater wonders would not our Saviour work in our regard!

Obstinacy in sin, my children, is a deliberate choosing of evil in preference to the Divine law—a deliberate surrender to Satan rather than to God. The Creator commands the creature to love Him with undivided heart and mind, and the latter perversely refuses to do so. What base ingratitude to an all-merciful Father! How many sinners at the present day continue their evil careers even to their last breath, presumptuously hoping for a death-bed repentance which may never be granted them. No wonder that God wearies of their obstinacy, no wonder that some are forsaken in the end.

A certain wealthy man who had obtained his vast wealth by unlawful means lay at the point of death. Seeing that there was no hope of recovery for him, he sent for his lawyer and witnesses that he might draw up his last will and testament before he died. When they approached his bedside, he, after a few preliminary remarks, began to dispose of his enormous wealth, ending with the fearful words: "My body I leave to the earth, from whence it came; my soul I surrender to Satan, to whom it belongs." Hardly believing his ears, the lawyer looked from one to the other of those surrounding the bedside, thinking that the dying man had lost his senses. As though divining the thought, however, the latter immediately added: "I still have the full use of my reason. Death has not as yet disabled me. I know the full import of all I am saying, yet, I repeat, my body I leave to earth, my soul to Satan." Though his friends used every effort to put him in a better frame of mind, the unfortunate man still persisted in his rash statement, giving this as the reason of his determination: "My whole life has been devoted to the service of the world—God has had no part in it. How, then, can I now offer Him my worthless soul? More than that, here before you all I bequeath to Satan not only my own soul, but also the souls of my wife and children. It is to please them that I have hoarded my ill-gotten wealth, to please them that I can no longer hope to see the face of my God!" Not long after he pronounced these terrible words the unhappy man expired in despair. Thus perish many poor souls who sacrifice their eternal salvation for the sake of the vain baubles of this world.

Remember, my children, that our dear Lord Himself testified that He came into this world not for the just but for sinners. Let us, each and every one, acknowledge ourselves sinners, but at the same time let us thank God He has given us a means of being reconciled to Him. The Sacrament of Penance is within the reach of all. Let us resort to it with contrite hearts, rejoicing that, no matter how enormous and shameful our spiritual infirmities, if we tell them to our Divine Lord, we shall be healed.

In the great city of Paris there lived a young student who unfortunately had led an evil life, but to whom God vouchsafed the grace of a sincere repentance. Going one day to the monastery of St. Victor, he fell at the feet of the Father Superior and begged to make his confession. He had only uttered a few words, however, when he suddenly grew silent, so great was the force of his sorrow. "Perhaps, my child," said the good priest, "if you would write your sins, you would be better able to confess them." The young man did as he was told. But again, as soon as he undertook the reading of the written words, his tears flowed so copiously that he could not continue. Then the confessor asked for the paper on which he had transcribed his wrongdoings. Upon reading this, the priest, having some doubt in his mind concerning the sins committed, asked leave of the penitent to seek the Abbot for advice. Permission being granted, what was the good priest's surprise when he unfolded the paper, to find every sign of writing obliterated. "This is most strange," he said to the Abbot, "only a moment ago I myself read the youth's entire confession from this paper." Having considered the matter, the two holy Fathers agreed that God by this miracle had been pleased to show that He had blotted all the young man's sins from the book of His remembrance, so great was the contrition.

May God spare each one of you, my children, from ever becoming a traitor to His law. Strive always to retain a conscience sensitive to the voice of grace. Be ever docile to its inspirations. And should you at times, perchance, succumb to the tempter through human frailty, have immediate recourse to the sweet Sacrament of Penance where God will meet you in loving sympathy. There, touching but the hem of His garment, you shall be healed.